7 5

Japanese
Poetic
Diaries

Published under the auspices of
The Center for Japanese and Korean Studies
University of California, Berkeley

Written or Edited by the Same Author
The Japanese Tradition in British and American Literature
Nihon o Utsusu Chiisana Kagami
Dryden's Poetry
The Fables of Aesop Paraphras'd in Verse by John Ogilby
Restoration Dramatists
Introduction to Japanese Court Poetry
The Works of John Dryden (*Associate General Editor*)

Written or Translated with Robert H. Brower
Japanese Court Poetry
Fujiwara Teika's Superior Poems of Our Time

Japanese Poetic Diaries

Selected and Translated,

with an Introduction,

by **Earl Miner**

UNIVERSITY OF CALIFORNIA PRESS
BERKELEY, LOS ANGELES, LONDON

University of California Press
Berkeley and Los Angeles, California

University of California Press, Ltd.
London, England

Designed by Steve Reoutt
Printed in the United States of America

For My Wife

Preface

For a Japanese there is a wealth of association to *nikki*, suggestions of art and high literary achievement that we do not imply by "diary." On the other hand, there is no fully current Japanese literary term equivalent to "poetic diary," a phrase I have coined to convey the special emphasis of the best Japanese literary diaries. But the form has existed, even if the term has not been current. And although *utanikki* (poetic diary) probably sounds unfamiliar to Japanese, it has in fact been used by Professors Konishi Jin'ichi in 1953 and Hisamatsu Sen'ichi in 1964 to describe works like those translated here. At all events, from A.D. 935 to the present there has been a continuous tradition of the literary diary, and the classics in the form have included poetry. The Introduction to this book seeks to define that tradition and to set forth the background, techniques, and meaning of the four diaries translated.

With one exception the diaries have been chosen for their merit, and especially the merit of the poetry in their prose contexts. All four were written by the greatest poets of their times—the tenth, eleventh, seventeenth, and very late nineteenth centuries. Such a time span makes them representative of social and literary tendencies over a period of more than ten centuries of Japanese literature. What the works reflect of their age is necessarily partial. *The Tosa Diary* has nothing explicit to say about politics and *The Diary of Izumi Shikibu* little about social structure. *The Narrow Road Through the Provinces* tells us very little of the rise of commercial classes or of city life, and *The Verse Record of My Peonies* has no comment on modern technological advances in Japan. But the same thing is true of comparable Western works, and closer examination would reveal that, after all, fundamental human and even social issues are raised. Love, time, and death are repeated subjects, and anyone wishing to know what important aspects of Japanese life were like through a millennium could find suggestions aplenty in these works. One treats of the family, another a love affair, yet another, life as a journey or as a feverish interval of illness; but each of these is in effect a major subject of human concern and something of a symbol of all that we strive for, or against, in our lives. So that although what the works reflect of their ages is necessarily partial, it is also very significant. The greatest distortion in such mirroring involves the considerable gaps between the four works, omissions of some very absorbing times and important works of Japanese literature. One must, therefore, not claim too much for what is reflected in these diaries. Yet of the poetic diary form itself one can say that it would probably be impossible to find another Japanese form practiced so continuously or mirroring so fully the dominant currents of national literature and its vision of human experience. The one form that excels it is of course poetry, but that is by definition included.

The exception to the rule that the diaries have ben selected for translation on the sole basis of merit is the last and briefest, *The Verse Record of My Peonies*. I should be hard pressed to argue that this is the finest of Shiki's poetic diaries. At the same time, none of its rivals has irresistible claims. But my real reason for choosing it, and indeed the beginning of this book, goes back twenty years, to a time in Nagoya when my friends, Mr. and Mrs. Nakagawa Saihei, gave me a lovely facsimile edition of Shiki's diary. At that time, and for a very long time afterwards, I was far more interested in the poems than in other features of the work. It is curious that the work has haunted me for two decades as a symbol of illness—as is natural enough, given the diary itself. I first recalled it when Mr. Nakagawa fell ill. Again, when in 1960 I visited Mrs. Nakagawa as she lay dying of cancer, Shiki's sufferings came forcibly to my mind. When in 1964 my wife had a serious operation, I took Shiki from the shelf and decided to translate it, as if to exorcise the spell. I can scarcely expect that others will have such strong personal associations with *The Verse Record of My Peonies*. Indeed, I hope they do not. But I also believe that it would not have affected me so deeply and unconsciously if it did not have a power and, I believe, a health that must be of value to every reader.

My wife recovered handsomely, and other preoccupations put the poetic diary from my mind. Thoughts of it returned in the summer of 1965 when, during a visit to England, I discussed with my friend Geoffrey Bownas some piece of work on Japanese literature that we might do together if, as I hoped, a Fulbright lectureship to Oxford University was forthcoming. We hit upon the idea of a book including four or five poetic diaries from early to modern times, deciding that each of us should go his own way and then bring to the common table what he had done. It has turned out, however, that the numerous duties connected with his professorship and the new Centre for Japanese Studies at Sheffield University have not allowed him time for translating. As a result, this is a book conceived and nurtured in illness, formed and trained in friendly conversations, and ended in pleasant solitary hours. Professor Bownas continued to play a role, however, with encouragement and advice.

I hope that such personal reflections will be allowed, if only because they serve to show that Japanese literature (like other literatures) speaks to us very personally, even when it is cast in a form unknown to our own literary traditions. My reasons for choosing the other diaries are no less personal, although they are less idiosyncratic: they are choices such as any student of Japanese diary literature would understand. But there are other works that might have been chosen instead, and therefore something may be said about the first three choices in this book. *The Tosa Diary* seemed an inevitable selection, because it is the first work in the form of the poetic diary—indeed, in all probability it is the first work of Japanese prose fiction; and to its originality of conception it adds such moving themes as a mother's love for her dead daughter. Such a concern is of the purest human significance, especially because it is presented with full scope for feeling but with-

out sentimentality. *The Diary of Izumi Shikibu* has a superior prose style, a beautiful succession of interspersed
poems, and the high romance of Japanese courtly love.
In it there emerges a woman who is at once one of the
finest Japanese poets and a lover to the point of abandon.
Her extraordinary passion is modulated by beauty into a
psychological fineness and subtlety that is representative
of Japanese art at its best. *The Narrow Road Through the
Provinces* is the greatest of the diaries included here, and
the greatest of all Japanese poetic diaries. Its account of
the beautiful places of northern and western Japan is one
I know to be moving even to those who have not seen
them, because I myself have never looked on Nikkō,
Matsushima, or Hiraizumi. But far more profound than
the journey in itself is the significance it carries. Travel is
a way of life, a restless existence pressed on by a consciousness of time at one's back and the prospect of death
ahead. The details of travel to the one side and the major
themes to the other are both touched upon by Bashō with
alternate humor, realism, wisdom, and sublimity. For such
reasons my choices are, if not inevitable, understandable.

My aim in the translations has been to make them accurate and natural. If there are inaccuracies, it is no fault
of the Japanese scholars I have relied upon, and if my
versions read unnaturally, the fault is likewise my own.
But I have sought to make the renderings accurate enough
for the scholar or his students and natural enough to appeal to readers whose interest is in pleasure from what
they read. (I do not for a moment think those two aims
necessarily opposed, but two kinds of readers are commonly involved.) The one kind of liberty I have repeatedly
taken with the original is the expansion or even introduction of words and phrases designed to show that a
given person said, whispered, wrote, or thought something. Such freedom with the original may have been a
mistake, since it deprives the diaries of some of their free
flow. But clarity seemed to me the first concern of the
translation. For the same reason, I have sometimes ex-
panded upon the text, but always as authorized by Japanese commentary. The translations are accompanied by

frequent notes. Some are addressed to the scholar, some to the general reader, and some to both. I have been encouraged to annotate with some frequency (though much more might have been included), because Japanese readers themselves appreciate or need such commentary, as the provision of it in editions for them shows. And a reader in Chicago or Manchester as well as Osaka may feel he deserves to know—because it means something to the work—if a given passage echoes some earlier Japanese or Chinese poet. Some notes, which will quickly be distinguished by their interpretive or personal character, originate with me, and the reader can therefore, if he chooses, regard them in a different light from the scholarly information taken out of Japanese editions. The Introduction is directed both to the scholar and the general reader, because it is much more interpretive and makes suggestions, whether right or wrong, that will sometimes not be found in Japanese scholarship.

My procedure in translating has been one insuring accuracy as far as possible. I have relied upon the Japanese scholars whose works are given in the Bibliographical Note and felt myself in good hands. At the same time, however, there are numerous cruces, controverted details, and debated issues in these diaries and the translator is often required to decide large matters as well as small by a choice from rival interpretations. More than that, as the Introduction makes clear, these four works have never been considered together before, and the concept of a tradition of diary literature continuing beyond 1350 is just emerging in Japan. My bringing them together and assuming such a tradition implies that I brought to them certain hypotheses, conclusions, feelings—call them what one will. It was necessary to refer these interpretations to someone who moved by second nature among the scholarship I was using and who could also encompass the range of my questions and beliefs. I therefore decided that my translations, and Introduction as well, would benefit from examination by my friend Professor Konishi Jin'ichi of Tokyo University of Education. At intervals for three years we have sent one way or another about the world manuscripts, new books, or letters concerned with poetic diaries. I am most grateful to him for the generous and wise help he has so unstintingly given me. It is typical of him that he should not only send me books, correct silly blunders, and become interested in my ideas, but also that he should share with me information and interpretations that he will be incorporating in subsequent works of his own. I fear that I have probably gone wrong on those matters over which I have disagreed with him or when I have not followed his advice. But working with him at distances as far from Tokyo as Los Angeles and Oxford has been one of many pleasures the book has brought me, and it is yet another to acknowledge the fact.

E. M.

OXFORD
March 1967

Acknowledgments

In addition to the material assistance given me by Professor Konishi, the aid of others has assisted me in this book. Mr. R. S. Dawson of Wadham College has generously assisted me in Chinese matters connected with Bashō's diary. Mr. Shimizu Shūyū, lector at Oxford before his return to Keiō University, has helped me with some historical details in *The Diary of Izumi Shikibu*. To the Warden and fellows of St. Antony's College I owe a debt for hospitality and privileges. The staff of the Oriental Institute at Oxford University has been unfailingly kind; and I am also grateful for the help given me, both *in situ* and through interlibrary loan, by the staff of the library of the School of Oriental and African Studies of the University of London. Before leaving for England, I also had the usual friendly assistance from the staff of the Oriental Library of the University of California, Los Angeles, and generous help from the East Asiatic Library of the University of California, Berkeley. I also wish to thank the Curators of the Oriental Institute at Oxford for putting at my disposal the very comfortable office of Professor David Hawkes, who generously seemed to think that it belonged to me rather than to him.

There are others to thank for permissions and assistance. The editor of *Japan Quarterly* has kindly allowed me to reprint *The Verse Record of My Peonies*, first published in his pages. Members of the editorial staffs of Kadokawa Shoten and Chikuma Shobō have assisted me in acquiring photographs for some of the illustrations in this book. Mr. Hasegawa Kichirō most graciously permitted me to reproduce portions of the famous screen illustrating Bashō's diary. Miss Mary Potter of The School of Geography, the University of Oxford, has drawn the maps, and Mr. Peter Suits of the Department of Printing and Production of my university has executed the drawing of the Tōsanjō Palace. Miss Jane Browne has very capably edited the manuscript of this book. My research assistant, Mr. John P. Loge, has also given me valuable help, and I have been assisted in reading proof by Mr. Ronald S. Baar and Mrs. Melanie Rangno. Finally, the Committee on Research of the University of California, Los Angeles has supported me with funds for this work, and it was completed while I held a Fulbright lectureship at Oxford.

It is a reflection of our dependence upon the generosity of others that I am indebted to these and perhaps yet other people for assistance on a book that really began, without my knowing it, twenty years ago with a gift from two friends, both of whom are now dead.

Contents

Names, Dates, and Abbreviations

Modern Japanese names are given in the Japanese order of surname and given name. (There are two exceptions where I have followed the order given on title pages.) The same pattern is followed for the appellations of earlier times, with "clan" or "house" names given first, then personal names or styles. When there have been alternatives, I have normally chosen one without calling attention to the others, especially for peripheral figures appearing in the footnotes. For the earlier period I have followed one common style of modern Japanese practice, giving the mediary *no* after the equivalent of surnames only when they were of one or two syllables: Ki no Tsurayuki, but Fujiwara Yasuhira.

All dates are from the Christian Era. The Introduction (see n. 1) discusses the handling of lunar dates, but in brief the lunar month is given by capital roman numerals, the day by arabic numerals, and the year by Western dating: VII. 7. 1004 is the date of the Tanabata Festival of the seventh night of the Seventh Month referred to in *The Diary of Izumi Shikibu*; by the solar calendar, it would already be August. The solar calendar is that used in *The Verse Record of My Peonies*.

Dates from the earlier period are often in dispute and usually approximate, even when not so indicated.

Abbreviations are used for the imperial anthologies and the early major collection, the *Man'yōshū*, with poems cited by anthology, scroll number, and poem number.

GSIS	*Goshūishū*	SGSIS	*Shingoshūishū*
GSS	*Gosenshū*	ShGSS	*Shokugosenshū*
KKS	*Kokinshū*	ShSZS	*Shokusenzaishū*

KYS	*Kin'yōshū*	SIS	*Shūishū*
MYS	*Man'yōshū*	SKKS	*Shinkokinshū*
	SZS	*Senzaishū*	

For descriptions of these and similar collections see the Appendix to Robert H. Brower and Earl Miner, *Japanese Court Poetry* (Stanford, 1961).

List of Illustrations

Introduction

Introduction

Diaries and Japanese Diary Literature

The convergence of two important human interests not only leads people to keep diaries, but also accounts for much of the interest diaries hold for readers. A diarist necessarily has a strong consciousness of time and a desire to memorialize what he has experienced. Many forms of history, of biography, and of literature are founded upon versions of the natural temporal order; but to the diarist, years, months, days, and even the hours of the day are the very basis of his writing. To the diarist's concern with temporal flow we may apply in a broader sense the oft-repeated phrase in Narcissus Luttrell's *Brief Relation*: "Time will shew." There are few people without an interest in what time shows in their lives, but the diarist goes beyond this interest: he wants to capture events in time by memorializing them in their sequence. He does consistently what some of us do on a voyage or at times of momentous events, and what some of us never do—he records the events he lives through, the people he encounters, and the thoughts he is prompted to. In acting as his own historian, the diarist is prompted by an interest in shorter time units than is the proper historian and is moved by a faith greater than that of the proper autobiographer in the efficacy of delineating such brief moments.

It is not certain whether the dual motivation to write diaries is felt by all peoples or by a people at all stages of its civilized development. But it is clear that among peoples impelled to write diaries Japanese and Anglo-Americans have responded prolifically. (The authoritative bibliography by William Matthews, *British Diaries* [Berkeley and Los Angeles, 1950] records about 2,500 in the

United Kingdom alone between 1442 and 1942. See also n. 38, below.) A contrast between the dominant interests of diarists in the two traditions will be useful to convey the special qualities of Japanese diary literature. To begin with, there is a distinction to be made between diarists: some respond more fully to public events, others to private. The public diary, or the journal as it may be called for convenience, was a form practiced as early as the eighth or ninth century by Japanese men setting down events in Chinese. Such diaries continued to be written for centuries. But the Japanese diaries that move toward literary modes are of another kind, private or diurnal. On balance, the great English diaries, those that have achieved the status of quasi-literature, are journals. Pepys' account of events such as the Great Fire of London, Evelyn's of the execution of Monmouth, or Defoe's mixed form, *The Journal of the Plague-Year*, are typical. Of course Pepys details features of his life in so personal a manner that he kept his diary in shorthand, but by comparison with the diary literature of Japan, his interests are "journalistic," or public. Japanese diarists of the kind considered in this book are more fully engaged with the diurnal experiences that concern themselves and people or matters within their personal ken. Their vision of what is most significant largely filters out those events that men share in a public context. In other words, Japanese diary literature usually concerns love rather than marriage, death rather than participation in mortal battles, the family rather than public life.

Such a general distinction requires a further discrimination, however, if the diary, whether journal or diurnal, is to achieve lasting interest. The English diary, which is in relative emphasis a public journal, demands for our interest a strong element of personal, private character. We expect a revelation at least of the diarist's personality if his record is to appeal to anyone other than a specialist in a bygone age. Pepys, the greatest English diarist, is absorbing to us precisely because his public design is so rich in an underlying personal pattern. The Japanese diurnal diary, which is in its relative emphasis a private record, must correspondingly accommodate matters of wider, more universal interest than those of a purely private individual if we are to read it with interest. The Japanese diarist may seek his universality by articulating common human concerns such as the family, love, death, nature, or time—but it is crucial for his success that he discover in diurnal, private events a universal significance or a thematic order growing above the mere sequence of daily activity.

The different basic emphases and the differing ways of transcending them for successful appeal to readers appear to arise from contrasting responses to the passage of time. To an English writer inheriting the Judaeo-Christian outlook modified by classical concerns, what is important in time is more-or-less great events, great actions in which men and women act as moral agents; that is, when they are responsible figures. To Japanese writers, with their dual inheritance of Shinto animism and Buddhist teaching, time is rather a natural cycle of nature to which man responds favorably on the whole or an immense flux of passing moments in a world caught in transient illusion but determined by karma. Whether English or Japanese, the writer is less apt to be conscious of these attitudes toward time than merely to accept, along with his readers, most of their features. The Western diarist is aware of time as events, the Japanese of time as a process. To the Japanese time is a flow, an experience of part of the flux of aeons in man's little while. Yet, to be successful, the two traditions must accommodate their basic emphases to each other to some extent. The English diarist must convey something like the Japanese immersion in process; at the least he must give a sense of movement, of development. Contrariwise, the Japanese must seek to arrest, if but for a moment, the transient stream, to catch the moment before the moon fades into the sky at dawn, to recall to life in one's memory the behavior of a child now dead, or re-create with the private imagination the splendors of those who once claimed the attention of the world. To put it crudely, the Westerner interested in setting forth his days is, as it were, in danger of remembering too much. (Proust may serve as an example.) And the Japanese is in danger of forgetting too much, as the elusive recording of days in Japanese diaries reveals.

To such numerous contrasts and distinctions we must add a further discrimination of the utmost importance to Japanese literature. So far the diaries considered have been what may be called natural diaries, the day-to-day jottings of events as they more-or-less actually occurred. But among Japanese diarists there are also those—and they are the ones represented in this book—who wrote art diaries in which fiction or a shaping along lines other than mere fact determines the nature of the creation and which, indeed, most readily allows the development of those larger themes that are essential for interest. The discrimination between Japanese natural and art diaries also sets the latter apart from Western diaries, because although what Pepys wrote may be more interesting than a given novel, and although he may have spent some care in shaping his events, we assume that he wrote fact and so react to his diary as a real record, not as a fiction. (It may well be that Pepys should be studied as an art diarist, but the fact is he has not been so read.) In Japan, on the other hand, there are some diaries so far fictional that they are included among the literary classics as works paralleling poems, plays, or novels.

It is certain that the Japanese believe that they have fictional or art diaries, and that we do not. But this is due less to any inherently superior sense of fiction than to their less rigid sense of what fiction is. When the dramatist Chikamatsu Monzaemon (1653–1725) wrote of the "narrow margin between truth and fiction," he spoke (though specifically about the drama) of a central feature of Japanese assumptions about literature. In the West, especially in the last half-century or so, we have come to think of a literary work as something existing autonomously, as a free creation untied to its circumstances of composition. The margin between truth and fiction we have supposed to be a very wide border. Japanese have leaned so far from the assumption that a work is divorced from its author or its circumstances that their first work of prose fiction, *The Tosa Diary*, is assumed to be an accurate record of weather and events in the voyage of Ki no Tsurayuki (869–945) from Tosa home to the capital. A glance at *The Verse Record of My Peonies*, also included here, will reveal that the homeliest, most convincingly factual details about an illness are included. Such assumptions are by no means confined to the diary. They apply to poetry, as a number of remarks in *The Tosa Diary* make clear. On the ninth of the Second Month the woman who is the narrator-diarist comments:

> I do not set down these words, nor did I compose the poem, out of mere love of writing. Surely both in China and Japan art is that which is created when we are unable to suppress our feelings.[1]

For the writer art is very clearly conceived of as a spontaneous overflow of powerful feeling about specific events in his own life. As a corollary, the reader, from at least certain kinds of literary works, will learn what has actually happened to someone and how the events affected the person involved in them. Such a conception is especially appropriate to Japanese art diaries, because most of them are based more wholly upon actual autobiographical events than any important Western literary work before this century. Yet the conception is far from being confined to the diary. There is a famous passage on the art of fiction in *The Tale of Genji* (*Genji Monogatari*). Prince Genji begins his discussion with a significant linking of the diary to prose fiction. He says to Tamakazura: "these diaries and romances which I see piled around you contain, I am sure, the most minute information about all sorts of people's private affairs." As if that were not enough, he continues in words very like, and no doubt intended to be like, Tsurayuki's. Fiction is written, he says,

---

[1] The lunar calendar used by Japanese till modern times fell progressively behind the solar sequence, so that its dates are confusing. The method used here is to give the month in capital roman numerals, the day in arabic numerals, and the year as in Western reckoning. Any other approach leads to a tangled web: XII. 4 of the 4th year of Manju was January 3, 1028 by our reckoning; but XII. 9 of the 1st year of Heiji was January 19, 1160. Translation from lunar to solar dates would also be awkward for such celebrations as those for the New Year. The form I have chosen may also retain something of the character of the original.

because the storyteller's own experience of men and things, whether for good or ill—not only what he has passed through himself, but even events which he has only witnessed or been told of—has moved him to an emotion so passionate that he can no longer keep it shut up in his heart. Again and again something in his own life or in that around him will seem to the writer so important that he cannot bear to let it pass into oblivion. There must never come a time, he feels, when men do not know about it.[2]

The interesting fact about this description of how literature comes to be written is that it is not used, as by itself it would seem to be, to describe a diary but rather a tale or romance (*monogatari*), and is included as part of a defense of *The Tale of Genji* itself, a work that, as far as we know, is not autobiographical. There is a clear assumption that a literary work is true to its author's life and times in a degree that is very Japanese, and very un-Western.

The "narrow margin between truth and fiction" is presumed to be much narrower, one can see, in Japanese literature. What, we may well ask, then distinguishes a Japanese art diary from a natural diary? The question is one only recently raised by Japanese scholars, and the very concept of "diary literature" or "literary diaries" (*nikki bungaku*) is only about fifty years old[3]—so strong had the assumption been that the "diaries" were actual records of events. Yet it is a marked fact that most of the important classical diaries avoid daily entries and obviously recall what has happened with great freedom. The most recent Japanese conclusion about the difference is, therefore, that although the natural diary is a record of fact, the art diary has in addition a "literary element"—more feeling, technique, style.[4] In short, even though there is a lesser degree of fiction in Japanese diary literature than in Western literature, there is an artistic reconstitution of fact participating in or paralleling fiction. So little is known about the authors of the earlier diaries that we are unable to ascertain how considerable the degree of artistic reshaping is. By the

---

[2] *The Tale of Genji*, trans. Arthur Waley (London, 1935), III, vii, 501.
[3] See Tamai Kōsuke, *Nikki Bungaku no Kenkyū* (Tokyo, 1965), p. 71.
[4] Tamai, *Nikki Bungaku no Kenkyū*, pp. 5–6, 70.

seventeenth century, or at least with *The Narrow Road Through the Provinces* of Matsuo Bashō (1644–1694), however, we are in a position to judge, because there still exists the *Diary* of his fellow-traveler, Iwanami Sora (1650–1711), which is a natural diary that may be compared with Bashō's art diary. Bashō is shown to have fictionalized, altered, and later revised.

However narrow the artistic margin, it proves to be very critical; it can be most conveniently represented by the fact that, almost without exception, the literary diaries from Heian to Muromachi times (in practice from *The Tosa Diary, ca.* 935 to *ca.* 1370) contain poems. One reason why the diaries include poems is that poems were in fact exchanged or written by the nobility to an extent unparalleled in any period in the West. Rapid, apposite composition was a necessary grace, as famous passages in *The Diary of Murasaki Shikibu* show. The powerful Fujiwara Michinaga (966–1027) from time to time pursued her at the court, and each of the adventures required a poem, often composed on the spot.[5] It was, therefore, much more natural—much more true to life—to include poems in a diary than it ever would have been in the West. And yet, the effect of the poems is to heighten the sense of fiction, the air of art, the presumption of literature. When a work averages two or three poems per page, the prose *continuo* must necessarily be in some degree answerable, and so it is likely to take on a more heightened artistic quality than prose without poems.

The frequent use of poems, the breaking away from the daily entry as a formal device, and a stylistic heightening —these are the chief symptoms of Japanese diary literature from classical to modern times. Not all diaries conform in all three respects, however, and some have the feel of being more fully determined by art—or by fact—than others. It must be said again that we simply lack sufficient evidence about the authors of most diaries to assess with assurance the preponderance of art or fact. But from what Japanese scholars feel as a conviction, we may ascertain

[5] See the quotations from her diary in Waley's Introduction to *The Tale of Genji*, pp. x–xi.

that the art diary is at once related to fact and freed by
art; it is like a balloon that whips about high in the air
while still attached to firm ground by a cable. The image
was used by Henry James for some of his own fiction, and
it is used here to stress both the attachment to fact and,
more strongly, the free floating of art in the Japanese
poetic diary.

A further distinction is possible among art diaries. There
are those relatively faithful to the immediate events they
set forth, and there are others that so far loosen the
Jamesian cable that they float with considerable freedom.
The former may be called recording diaries (*jiroku nikki*),
the latter narrative diaries (*tsukuri nikki*), and the distinction is the more natural for being one that Japanese scholars make among tales (*monogatari*). In this sense, the
Ōkagami (*ca.* 1115) is a recording tale (*jiroku monogatari*), dealing, albeit with the art of a fictional dialogue,
with actual historical events. By contrast, *The Tale of
Genji* is a narrative tale (*tsukuri monogatari*), borrowing
from history and real social custom but dedicated to a fully
developed fiction. It is so for the art diaries. *The Diary of
Murasaki Shikibu* is beautifully written and ordered by
poems and such devices as galleries of character-portraits,
but it is a recording diary by virtue of its fidelity to actual
events and personalities. *The Tosa Diary,* on the other
hand, however accurately it may mirror the experience of
an actual voyage, is committed to a narrative freed from
fact by its creation of fictional characters. Significantly, the
preponderance of poems is greater—and their quality
usually higher—in the narrative diary. It will be quickly
seen that such a distinction between kinds of art diaries
implies that the materials treated, the situation delineated,
and the narrative point of view are apt to differ in the two
kinds. It is not necessary to pursue such differences here,
however, partly because they require minute analysis of
numerous works, but more especially because the diaries
translated for this book are narrative diaries whose techniques are best discussed in sections of separate consideration for each diary.

Other features of the art diary can be explained by discussion of the history of its development and its relation to other forms. The earliest Japanese diaries were natural diaries, kept by men and written in Chinese. It was by turning from Chinese as the medium and from a concern with public events that the art diary, and with it prose fiction, took shape in Japan. Although this development took place much earlier in Japan than in England, in the tenth rather than the eighteenth century, it bears a striking resemblance to the sudden growth of the English novel once an epistolary convention was established. The Japanese transition from fact to art is of course in the diary rather than the letter, and it is made very explicitly in the first sentence of *The Tosa Diary*: "It is said that diaries are kept by men, but I shall see if a woman cannot also keep one." The shift was made from Chinese to Japanese, from male to female diarists—and from fact to fiction, because the author is a man using the narrative point of view of a woman. This pose of Tsurayuki's was remarkably prescient. Throughout the eleventh century, diaries and other successful literary forms in Japanese were, at least in terms of highest quality, the property of women.

The Tosa Diary maintained the daily-entry form of the Chinese diaries kept by men—the form of modern natural diaries.[6] Subsequent diarists gave up the daily-entry form and, instead, might pass over long periods of time with a phrase or, on the other hand, devote to a single night the most detailed description. (The question how a work called a diary can be based upon any form other than that of daily-entry must be deferred.) Such a manipulation of time required some other plot or continuum to take the place of the regular sequence that had been displaced. One common form is the travel record such as is found in *The Tosa Diary* or *The Diary of the Waning Moon*.[7] Another form approaches plot by relating a continuing action such as a love affair, using its development as a basis of whole-

---

[6] The comparison is drawn by Imai Takauji, *Heian Jidai Nikki Bungaku no Kenkyū* (Tokyo, 1957), pp. 151–152.

[7] The latter, *Isayoi Nikki, ca.* 1280, composed by Nun Abutsu (d. 1283), tells of her journey to the Kamakura shogunate. It is included in Edwin O. Reischauer and Joseph K. Yamagiwa, *Translations from Early Japanese Literature* (Cambridge, Mass., 1951), pp. 52–119.

ness. *The Diary of Izumi Shikibu* and *The Tale of Takamura* (also called *The Diary of Takamura*) are examples
of this form.[8] Yet another form seeks to give the tenor of
a lifetime, even if the time span is shorter than a whole
life. There are three major examples of this form: *The
Diary of Murasaki Shikibu*, telling of life at court; *The
Sarashina Diary*, recounting the maturation and adult life
of a girl from the provinces; and *The Gossamer Diary*, describing "what the life of a well-placed lady is really like."[9]
It can be seen that, having given up the daily-entry form,
the art diary moved to forms not unlike those of the short
story or novel.

Japanese studies of diary literature end with the fourteenth century, although Japanese scholars are well aware
of such later works as *The Diary of Masahiro* (*Masahiro
Nikki*) of Ichijō Kaneyoshi (1402–1481). What compli-
cates the matter is that the subgenre of the travel diary
or travel record (*kikō*), which emerged in the mid-
thirteenth century, assumed such importance that the
larger class designated as the diary (*nikki*) gradually
yielded to its subclass. As the selections in this book show,
that view is not inevitable. There appear to be several
reasons for the conventional terminal date for diary literature. The period during which most of the classical works
were written and either then or later given the name diary
in their title was the period from the tenth to the fourteenth century. The dominance by women of prose fiction
did not survive even to the fourteenth century. From the
fifteenth or sixteenth-century authors come from new social groups, and they compose in new poetic forms.
Whereas earlier diarists had written in the *waka*, or *tanka*,

---

[8] *The Diary of Izumi Shikibu* is included in this book. There is no
translation of the latter work. Ono no Takamura (802–852) was a poet,
and fourteen of the thirty-two poems in the *Tale* (or *Diary*) are by him.
Its character can be conveyed by its opening: "There once was a young
woman who had been reared by her parents with great care."

[9] *The Diary of Murasaki Shikibu* (*Murasaki Shikibu Nikki*) and *The
Sarashina Diary* (*Sarashina Nikki*) will be found (with *The Diary of
Izumi Shikibu*) in Annie Shepley Omori and Kochi Doi, *Diaries of Court
Ladies of Old Japan* (Tokyo, 1935, 1961). *The Gossamer Diary* (*Kagerō
Nikki*) is very ably translated by Edward Seidensticker (Tokyo, 1964).

FIG. 3. Matsuo Bashō
*From a portrait by Ogawa Haryū (1663–1747), painter
and disciple of Bashō. This is one of the most
authentic portraits.*

Courtesy of Professor Konishi Jin'ichi

form, diarists gradually come to use *haikai* poetry, and by the modern period, *haiku*. The *tanka* is a five-line form in 5–7–5–7–7 syllables. Originally *haikai* were linked verses in which several poets work together composing 5–7–5 or 7–7 stanzas in alternation, usually making a series of thirty-six or a hundred. But *haikai* is also used more loosely to mean verse, and especially the crucial opening verse (*hokku*, 5–7–5) from a full *haikai*. There is the presumption that more stanzas will be added. But in practice *hokku* were often composed to stand alone, like *haiku*, a form of 5–7–5 syllables with no supposition of addition being necessary.[10] It is by reason of such social and literary changes that formal Japanese accounts of diary literature end where they do, omitting to follow the conception into the Tokugawa period (1603–1867) or modern times. New terms are apt to be invented. The minglings of prose and *haikai* by Bashō and other Tokugawa writers are usually characterized as *haibun*, "*haikai* prose," or "*haikai* literature." Commonly, works following natural chronology and so making some sort of record are designated by a word ending in -*ki*, "record" (cf. *nikki*, "daily record" or diary).

Yet to insist upon the continuity of diary literature is not to introduce Western ingenuity into study of Japanese literature. In a very significant passage, Bashō wrote of a continuing tradition from Tsurayuki to his own time, a tradition he designated as "diaries of the road" (*michi no nikki*).[11] Moreover, in recent years certain Japanese scholars have started to relate art diaries of various periods. The first attempt to relate early with "feudal" diaries was apparently that of Professor Konishi Jin'ichi, who must have startled readers by declaring flatly in the opening sentence of the Introduction to his edition of *The Tosa*

---

[10] The first usage of "*haiku*" (evidently from *haikai no ku*) dates from 1663. The term appears throughout the next two centuries but is relatively rare. Bashō uses *haikai*. *Haikai* was originally conceived of as the humorous form of *renga*—a one-hundred-stanza sequence of the same verse form. The linked *haikai* of Bashō and other "feudal" poets is often called *renku* today. Although *haiku* were, in effect if not in name, composed earlier, they did not supersede *haikai* as the supposed norm until the Meiji period (1868–1912).

[11] See below, p. 42, for full quotation and citation.

Diary: "*The Tosa Diary* is *haikai* literature."[12] By this he
implies more detailed resemblance than need be examined
here, but the association of two works previously thought
to be distinct in genre set an important precedent. Professor Tamai Kōsuke refers to Professor Konishi's comment, but it seems to me he misses the major point of it,
thinking that all that is meant is that *The Tosa Diary* shows
wit and humor. Still Professor Tamai remarks on his own
that what he calls diary literature has continued to be
written past the fourteenth century to the present. He
ends at the conventional date only because he feels that
insufficient research has been done on the subject in the
period after the fourteenth century.[13] At all events, if
we define for ourselves the poetic diary as a form allowing for use of *waka, haikai, haiku,* or free verse, and if we
allow for as much freedom in the handling of time as is
traditionally allowed to the early diary literature, then
we can indeed trace the form without effort from *The
Tosa Diary* of about 935 to the present. It is easier to arrive
at such a conception in English, because, paradoxically,
our minds are not conditioned by historical associations
with specific works referred to as diaries (*nikki*). And although the definition implied by this book seems radical,
it follows both Bashō and recent scholarship sufficiently
to arouse no objection from Japanese scholars.

Perhaps the chief reason why many Japanese scholars
have not followed the development of the diary beyond
the fourteenth century is that so many problems of definition affect the earlier diary. It will quickly be understood
that, once writers left the daily-entry form of the natural
diary and wrote with seeming indifference to the regular
passage of time, they were likely to end with forms of ambiguous connection with the diary mode as it is generally
understood. It is in fact no simple task to answer the question, What do Japanese think a literary diary is? *The
Tosa Diary* is a simple case: it was never called anything

---

[12] Konishi Jin'ichi, *Tosa Nikki Hyōkai* (Tokyo, 1951, 1965), p. 1. Professor Konishi is preparing a new edition of this work and has very kindly
discussed matters general and detailed with me.

[13] Tamai, *Nikki Bungaku no Kenkyū*, pp. 70, 105–106.

but a diary, and it maintained the daily-entry form. Other works, however, may also be called personal poetic collections (*kashū*) or tales, romances (*monogatari*). Yet other titles were devised. The following table will suggest how complicated the matter is.

DATE	USUAL TITLE	OTHER TITLES	TRAVEL FORM	DAILY-ENTRY FORM
935	*Tosa Nikki* (*The Tosa Diary*)	none	yes	yes
945	*Ise Monogatari* (*The Tales of Ise*)	*Zaigo Chūjō Nikki*, etc. (*Diary of Middle Commander Zaigo*)	no	no
962	*Takamitsu Nikki* (*The Diary of Takamitsu*)	*Tōnomine Shōshō Monogatari* (*The Tale of the Tōnomine Lieutenant*)	no	no
?965	*Heichū Monogatari* (*The Tale of Heichū*)	*Sadafun Nikki* (*The Diary of Sadafun*)	no	no
974	*Kagerō Nikki* (*The Gossamer Diary*)	None. But often compared to *monogatari*	no	no
?1005	*Izumi Shikibu Nikki* (*The Diary of Izumi Shikibu*)	*Izumi Shikibu Monogatari* (*The Tale of Izumi Shikibu*)	no	no
After 1210	*Ono no Takamurashū* (*Collection of Ono no Takamura*)	*Takamura Monogatari* (*The Tale of Takamura*), *Takamura Nikki* (*The Diary of Takamura*)	no	no
1232	*Kenrei Mon'in Ukyō no Daibushū*	None. But sometimes referred to as a diary.	no	no
1280	*Isayoi Nikki* (*The Diary of the Waning Moon*)	*Abutsu Michiyuki*, etc. (*The Travels of Abutsu*)	yes	no
1370	*Michiyukiburi* (*Travelings*)	none	yes	no

In other words, some works called diaries are also called tales (*monogatari*), collections (*-shū*, *kashū*), records (*-ki*), travels (*michiyuki*), and yet other names. Equally, tales are often called diaries. One can go farther.[14] There were diaries of poetry matches (*utaawase*), which were themselves a distinct form. The historical tales (*rekishi-monogatari*) such as *Ōkagami* (*The Great Mirror*) were sometimes called diaries and, like the other forms men-

[14] The rest of the paragraph is greatly indebted to Tamai, *Nikki Bungaku no Kenkyū*, pp. 50–70.

tioned, contained poems. Finally, there are numerous re-
semblances between the diary and such Japanese pensées
(*zuihitsu*) as *The Pillow Book* (*Makura no Sōshi*) of Sei
Shōnagon.

Two conclusions stand out clearly from this description.
Any work called a diary, that is, which is an art diary—or
even works associated with it but given a different generic
name—contains poems. And the conception of the diary,
however dim, is the basic literary conception of prose fiction from 935 to 1370. The poems vary in number and
importance with the individual work, depending in considerable part on whether it is a narrative or recording
diary, but it seems clear that poetry is conceived of as the
most basic or purest literary form and that its presence,
almost alone, is enough to change a journal of one's life
to an art diary. More than that, to a writer of the court
period, prose fiction appears to have been impossible without poetry. The evidence is too consistent for one to argue
that by including poems the authors were merely reflecting the customs of the day; and often the poems are not
exchanges at all but lyric overflowings in solitude on some
subject. It is poetry that proves the artistic nature of the
whole, distinguishing it from a natural diary or other factual record, whether the distinction be as simple as that
in *The Tosa Diary* or as complex as the nearly eight hundred poems of *The Tale of Genji*, the nearly one hundred
of *The Tale of the Heike* (*Heike Monogatari*), or the ap-
proximately 150 of *The Mirror of the Present* (*Imaka-
gami*), all of which are often considered in terms of
prose alone.

Such a view of the importance of poetry is demonstrated, moreover, by examination of the diaries and related works. Whether or not we accept the view that the
intent of *The Tosa Diary* is to teach the art of poetry,[15]
it is an eloquent statement on the importance of the art.
Or again, in *The Diary of Izumi Shikibu*, we notice that
repeatedly it is the Lady's responsiveness to the world in

---

[15] The view is Tamai's, *Nikki Bungaku no Kenkyū*, p. 104. The relation
between poetry and prose in the diaries is discussed below under the
heading *Poetry and Diaries*.

a poem that brings back the Prince's wandering affection. Throughout this earlier period of Japanese literature poetry defines classic literature of all important genres. There are not scholarly aids to Tokugawa fiction as there are for works in the earlier period, so it is more difficult to generalize about such matters as the proportion of poetry and prose in Tokugawa and modern diaries. Even so, examination of *The Narrow Road Through the Provinces* or of *The Verse Record of My Peonies* suggests that, however beautiful or pedestrian the diary prose may become, in the seventeenth or late nineteenth centuries the poems remain as central as in the earlier diaries.

The other significant inference—that the diary is the representative and indeed normative form of classical prose fiction—is one that suggests the extent to which literature was regarded as an expression of the flow of experience of an individual author. The defense of the art of fiction in *The Tale of Genji* has already been shown to be closely related to the diary and indeed to echo the ideas of Tsurayuki in the *Tosa Nikki* and in his Preface to the *Kokinshū*.[16] If the diary has such importance to prose fiction of several kinds, that is because it gave most significant expression to the Japanese interest in, or obsession with, time. In this respect, the diary is to prose fiction what seasonal poems are to the imperial collections: the most characteristic and important, not necessarily in quality, but in conveying the kind of experience felt to be significant. The seasonal poems themselves were organized on a temporal progression from the beginning to the end of the year, the order of poems being arranged both by observed sequence in the occurrence of natural phenomena and by the sequence of social events in the *Annual Ceremonial* (*Nenchū Gyōji*). The diary is likewise bound to temporal progression, whether of the hours of the day, the days of the week, the months of the year, or even the years of a lifetime. As a form, however, it did not need to bind itself to daily entries. The higher ripples and waves in the stream of time were more important to diary litera-

---

[16] The *Kokinshū* is the first of the imperial anthologies, compiled by Tsurayuki and others about 905.

ture than lesser units, because they gave shape to the pressure of the stream.

The later diaries included in this book show not only the same primacy of poetry as the earlier but also the same sense of temporal flow. Bashō begins his *Narrow Road Through the Provinces* with a prose poem on time, and his most profound passages are those resonant with the music of time. In *The Verse Record of My Peonies*, Masaoka Shiki (1867–1902) is conscious of each moment of his life, knowing that he is close to death. In such a state he notices changes of light or the number of petals of flowers, and he imagines his last moments. The literary evidence has not been ordered, but it must be said that if Bashō and Shiki are representative, the feudal and the modern poetic diary reveal the same dominant features as the earlier diaries: a normative role for poetry and an awareness of time.

The significance of these two elements is such that without an appreciation of them we are unlikely to gain any adequate feel for Japanese diary literature. Compared with Western fiction, the diary is seemingly episodic and formless, and where, some may ask, is the firm plot of *Tom Jones* or of *Middlemarch?* The answer is that there is no firm plot in the diaries—nor in other forms of earlier Japanese prose fiction, not in drama, and not in modern fiction.[17] Japanese conceptions of form are in some important respects different from Western, and what the differences are can be understood in considerable measure from the diary. One of the significant differences between Western and Japanese prose fiction (as represented by the diary) is that the Japanese emerges so much earlier in the society's development than does fiction in the West. Another is that it is formulated in close relationship to poetry, which both affects its principles of coherence and means that it did not need to go through the stage of the well-

---

[17] In recent years Japanese scholars of diary literature have drawn the comparison between art diaries and the so-called "I-novel" (*shishōsetsu*) of modern Japanese fiction, which usually presents veiled autobiographical detail as fiction.

made novel or play before it could seek out freer forms. To attempt generalization of a large number of works, the diaries combine, or poise, two formal energies: the ceaseless pressure of time implied by the diary form itself and the enhancement of the moment, or related moments, usually demonstrated in poetry. It is the flow of time rather than the concatenation of events or architecture of design that is important, and the sudden glowing of poetic experience rather than the order of a well-lighted city that gives the diaries their sense of depth of experience.

Poetry and time are also the two chief thematic bases of the diaries. After prose has said all it can, or all that it is decent for it to attempt, poems rise to have their say. It is as though Tsurayuki were merely factual in saying that Japanese were spontaneously given to song and that poetry rose from particularly strong feeling. With the exception of the unsatisfactory conclusion of *The Diary of Izumi Shikibu* (which violates the point of view and the major concern of the work), each of the diaries included here can be as well understood as a poetic whole joined by prose as a prose work interspersed with poems. The prose of the diary is not merely an excuse for the poem; but the poems are not also a mere decoration. It is their canons of taste, their associations and assumptions, and their themes that the diaries develop. This much can be shown by comparison of the diaries with the imperial collections, or more easily by concern with the basic themes of the works. Of the four diaries included here all but *The Diary of Izumi Shikibu* are concerned with death, and that describes life as a dream. The connection between time and death needs no special explanation, and what is required may be dealt with in respect to separate works. But dream is the central metaphor for the essential experience of Japanese courtly love,[18] and it is related to Buddhist ideas about the illusory nature of experience in this world. The sense of annihilation or desolation, of dream, and of celebration of life are basic to Japanese poetic re-

---

[18] See my "Japanese and Western Images of Courtly Love," *Yearbook of Comparative and General Literature,* XV (1966), 174–179.

sponses, and basic as well to these diaries.[19] Both the joy and the deprivation, like the essentially poetic disposition of the works, give the diaries an appeal that is no less human for taking forms of expression in some ways at variance from those of other literatures.

The Tosa Diary

The Tale of the Bamboo Cutter (*Taketori Monogatari*) has long been called by Japanese scholars "the parent of all tales." But *The Tosa Diary* may properly be termed the parent of all Japanese prose fiction, including the tale, since, according to recent opinions of Japanese scholars, it precedes *The Tale of the Bamboo Cutter* by about a quarter of a century. It seems almost certainly to be the first work of Japanese prose fiction extant. There can be no doubt of its prime historical importance, although its intrinsic literary worth is not so high. The *Diary* (*Tosa Nikki* or, properly, *Tosa no Niki*) purports to be an account by a woman of her return to the capital, what is now Kyoto, in the party of the man who had been governor for some time of Tosa Province, now southern Shikoku (see fig. 6). The details of the return are in many respects so particular and factual that one can only conclude that as a fictional work the *Diary* was reconstituted from a natural diary kept by the author, Ki no Tsurayuki, or by someone in his party. Tsurayuki (869–945)[20] was appointed governor of Tosa early in 930 and went to the province in the early autumn. He completed his duty and left for the capital at the end of 934, arriving in early spring, 935. It is presumed that the *Diary* was written in its present art form some time during 935. It quickly became known as

---

[19] On such elements in Japanese poetry, see my *Introduction to Japanese Court Poetry* (Stanford, 1968), Chaps. I and VIII.

[20] Dates and most other facts in what follows are fairly well established. For such matters my account is indebted to Tamai, *Nikki Bungaku no Kenkyū*, pp. 85–108, and Suzuki in the introductory matter to his *Tosa Nikki*, etc. For criticism and interpretation, my account is indebted to Professor Konishi, both in his edition of the work and in his correspondence. See the Bibliographical Note.

Tsurayuki's, and poems from it were credited to him by compilers of imperial anthologies and by others who had occasion to state the authorship of such poems used as examples.

By contemporary standards, Tsurayuki was an old man in 935—he was sixty-six. His had been a career highly distinguished in literary matters, although he was by no means brilliant as a courtier. To the really important nobility, appointment as a mere governor of a province would have been thought a disgrace. For a middling courtier like Tsurayuki on the other hand, however much he would regret leaving the capital, it would have been a profitable post. This much is clear both from his origins in a scholarly family and from nearly contemporary comments on the wealth to be gained from the governorship of a province. The *Diary* jokes about it on I. 4: "we have become—ever so wealthy." Not a great deal is known of Tsurayuki's first thirty-five years or so, but in 905 he and three other men finished the compilation of the first imperial collection, the *Kokinshū*. It was this achievement that appears to have brought him the admiration of his contemporaries (although to some extent it must also have been a recognition of his previous status), because thereafter he figures more prominently in records of poetry matches, in composition of poems for screens, and in other appointments for which poetic prestige was a requisite for anyone without higher rank. Comments about him by his fellow compilers suggest that he was their leading figure, and certainly it was he who wrote the important Japanese Preface of the work, which assisted in making him the most famous literary figure of his day and one of the central figures in the history of Japanese poetry.

The Preface is of great significance in itself and is one of Tsurayuki's "first's" in Japanese literary history. No extended work of Japanese literary criticism had preceded it, and criticism in subsequent centuries is heavily indebted to it. Its connections with themes of *The Tosa Diary* will be dealt with subsequently, but there is another important connection—the Preface is the first significant piece of Japanese prose written in the medium

that was to become that of the *Diary* and of subsequent
prose fiction for centuries. This medium is termed *wabun*
(Japanese composition as opposed to Chinese) or *kanabun*
(composition in—or largely in—the phonetic syllabary as
distinct from Chinese characters). It has already been
observed that the temporal progression given to seasonal
(and, it may be added, to love) poems by Tsurayuki and
his colleagues relates to the diaries' concern with time. It is
also true that their efforts to discover the biographical
situation of a poem, or to recover the circumstances of
composition, and then to put such matters into a headnote
reveal a tendency to think of what may be called the
prose contexts of poems. The tendency is a very old one.
The headnotes or footnotes added by Ōtomo Yakamochi
(718–785) to his poems in the *Man'yōshū*, the great early
collection of poetry, seem almost to be excerpts from a continuing diary (see especially numbers 4139 ff. in Book XIX
or 4011–4015 and their prose footnote in XVII).

Such matters lie behind the *Diary* and may help explain
how Tsurayuki might have come to write the first work
of Japanese prose fiction. But there are numerous uncer-
tainties, and among them dispute over the degree of fiction in the *Diary*. (It is only fair to say that the remarks
following diverge from usual Japanese views.) The problem is partly that it is so convincingly circumstantial and
particular, at times seemingly artless, that Japanese and
other readers can only take it as a record growing inte-
grally from the actual experience of voyage. What has
rendered such an interpretation difficult to some is that
the first sentence of the *Diary* makes clear that it is nar-
rated or "kept" by a woman. This technique—a brilliant
breakthrough in narrative point of view for a first work
of fiction—and the fact that subsequent *kana*-literature
is a medium dominated by women have led some Japanese
(as recently as 1956) to say that the *Diary* was probably
written by Tsurayuki's wife. What that view utterly misses
is the immense step of Tsurayuki's imagination in creating
a wholly fictional narrator and first-person narration. It is
of course possible that the woman narrator is modeled
on "Tsurayuki's wife," but nothing is known of her or of

that child of the woman narrator who is said to have been born in the capital and to have died in Tosa. If that child was his, it was born when he was over sixty. Whether or not the woman narrator is based on Tsurayuki's wife simply cannot be discovered. We do not know if he had one, or more than one, or any at the time. What is clear is that she is a free creation detached in her own consciousness from the other passengers. Numerous slight details suggest that she is either the wife of the ex-governor (Tsurayuki's version of himself) or someone very high in his entourage. She is mistress of what appears to be the house to which the main body of the entourage returns, and therefore apparently of the ex-governor's house. But the connection is never made, and it is such teasing, tenuous, and unprovable relations between fact and fiction that have caused the critical mischief.

The prominence of the woman narrator is indisputable, but application of the principle of the narrative point of view is less easy. Although in general Tsurayuki maintains a remarkable consistency of narrative viewpoint, there are moments when we very definitely seem to be shifted out of the woman's consciousness into an impersonal, or omniscient, narration. In the second paragraph of I. 9, for example, we read, "the people standing on the shore have grown remote," which follows the woman's consciousness; but then we read, "and the people aboard the ship have grown out of sight of those on land" (*fune no hito mo miezu narinu*). It may be that what is implied is "*we* people aboard the ship," but the personal nouns equivalent to personal pronouns in English are seldom used, and the effect of such passages is that of a shift in point of view. These instances are relatively rare, however, and seldom cause real difficulty. In English it is far harder to convey for the four diaries included here the sense of differing effects achieved by changing techniques, as it were, of not using personal pronouns. Just as our specification can do different things, so the lack of specification in Japanese can at times imply clearly who is speaking, at other times leave the matter open; it can suggest that what is written is speech, or thought, or something between. Who speaks or thinks may be made clear, or not specified. Generally speaking, the result is that actors become much less important than actions, thinkers than thoughts, and feelers than feelings. It is the experience that is of crucial importance and that achieves a fuller verbal expression than in English.

The absence of certain kinds of clear specification lies behind yet another problem, the identity of the three chief male characters. There is the rather crude captain, there is the ex-governor, and there is someone called *funagimi*, "lord of the boat." Most Japanese scholars take the *funagimi* to be the ex-governor, which is a very natural interpretation. And yet on XII. 26 the ex-governor is shown to be a skillful poet, whereas on II. 7, the *funagimi* is said to be ignorant of poetry.[21] It seems likely that the *funagimi* is a third character, a kind of guide heading up the party of the ex-governor, and he is therefore given in the translation as "our leader" or "the leader of us passengers."

Yet a more difficult problem involving the characters is the authorship of the poems during the journey. As Tsurayuki's contemporaries knew, though some modern scholars have confused themselves on the issue, he is the *author* of all the poems. That is not the question. Rather, we must often ask who it is among the fictional characters on the voyage who is imagined to have composed an individual poem. A large proportion of the poems are simply said to be by "someone" on the boat. I suspect that some of these are poems that Tsurayuki found it difficult to attribute to any specific person among his identified characters, and some may be poems which he had composed *in propria persona* on the actual journey home. But I also believe that in a number of cases "someone" is a polite equivalent for the fictional narrator, the woman, and I have therefore given to her a very few poems not so given by Japanese editors. My own inclination would be to attribute many of such poems to her, but I have

---

[21] I owe the distinction to a letter from Professor Konishi. But there seem in any event to be some inconsistencies, e.g., on II. 6 the travelers are surprised that the Old Woman of Awaji could compose a poem, though she had already done so on I. 26.

contented myself with doing so only when there seemed little doubt. On I. 11, for example, the second poem is given to the woman narrator, although the Japanese reads *hito no yomeru,* "someone wrote." The fact that the poem concerns the narrator's dead girl makes it impossible that anyone else among the fictional characters we are given could have written the poem. In certain other respects as well, I have brought forward the woman's personality or identity to an extent that many Japanese scholars might find surprising.

Apart from such problems, the characters are economically but clearly developed. In addition to those already mentioned, there is the seasick Old Woman of Awaji, who surprises everyone with a spirited poem. There are also children or young people for whom Tsurayuki writes poems that are dramatically appropriate. The most interesting minor characters appear on I. 7, at Ōminato, where we have the finest example in this *Diary* of that humor which sparkles with one color of light or another in all four pieces included in this book. On that day there appears at the boat a bumpkin laureate who wishes to show the people of the capital his prowess at poetry. The woman promises to remember his name but never tells us. The bard comes with a cabinet full of fine food—the present is obviously an excuse to recite a poem he has put together. To make his poem seem appropriate he mentions, what everybody knows, that the waves are running high. The poem, which he recites in a very loud voice, is so foolish that no one replies, and everyone eats what he brought while he sulks till dark. Such humorous characterization is accompanied by witty plays on words and other touches giving a bright thread to the story. And yet, as so commonly in Japanese literature, the tone shifts markedly at the end of the episode, when a small child volunteers, in spite of shyness, to recite a poem for the local bard, who had however already left the boatside. So the attention of the passengers turns with affectionate scrutiny to the child. Simple episodes like this often convey greater humanity than more pretentious ones.

By far the most important character, however, is the

woman, who is not only the technical center of narration

woman, who is not only the technical center of narration
but also the center of human interest. It is through her
that Tsurayuki develops his two principal themes—the
centrality of art to life, and the tragedy of existence. The
former is clearly raised on I. 9 and 20 and on II. 9 and 16.[22]
The explicit postulate is that human beings write naturally,
spontaneously, from powerful feelings aroused by what
they encounter and love in the world. Tsurayuki had
said as much in the opening words of his Preface to the
Kokinshū.

> The poetry of Japan has its roots in the human heart and
> flourishes in the countless leaves of words. Because human
> beings possess interests of so many kinds, it is in poetry
> that they give expresion to the meditations of their hearts
> in terms of the sights appearing before their eyes and the
> sounds coming to their ears. Hearing the warbler sing
> among the blossoms and the frog in his fresh waters—is there
> any living being not given to song? It is poetry which, with-
> out exertion, moves heaven and earth, stirs the feelings of
> gods and spirits invisible to the eye, softens the relations
> between men and women, calms the hearts of fierce warriors.

Clearly, such a conception of the naturalness of poetry is
a central article of faith to Tsurayuki. And yet with it goes
another belief to which it must be accommodated if his
thought and practice are to be understood.

We can approach that belief by remarking that Japanese scholars have long since pointed to a change from the
style of poetry practiced by Tsurayuki in the *Kokinshū* to
that thirty years later in the *Diary.* The earlier style is
commonly highly wrought, artful, the later usually simpler.[23] Such alteration has led many Japanese scholars to
believe that late in life Tsurayuki revised his ideas about
the proper style of poetry, turning his back on the artful
techniques of his earlier years and welcoming instead an
unaffected, simpler way of writing. Unfortunately, the

---

[22] See nn. 9 and 26 to the translation.
[23] See Robert H. Brower and Earl Miner, *Japanese Court Poetry* (Stanford, 1961), Chap. V, on the style of Tsurayuki and the Early Classical
Period. The translation of the opening of the Preface is taken from
Japanese Court Poetry.

problem is not so easy. In the *Kokinshū*, Tsurayuki's poems are signed "Tsurayuki," but in the *Diary* they are attributed to this or that fictional character. Tsurayuki could not write for the bard of Ōminato or the Old Woman of Awaji as he would in his own person. The poems are "naturally" simpler because they are made to fit rather ordinary poetic talents; they are also "artificially" simpler in being creations that will be appropriate for the individual characters of the journey. It must be added, however, that certain factors complicate the view that the poems are wholly "dramatic." Some are written with great art and others would easily pass muster as formal poems with slight changes of diction. It seems most temperate to conclude that the poems are, with some exceptions, intended to be "dramatically" appropriate to characters in the *Diary*, but that some "dramatic" occasions are sufficiently formal to produce formal verse. Although the issue has not, to my knowledge, been raised, the change in prose style from the Preface of the *Kokinshū* to the *Diary* may also be considered. The earlier work has a studied, brilliant style of great variety and rich texture. The later work is written in a far simpler, almost unadorned style. Our conclusion about the change can only be the same as for the poems. In the *Diary*, Tsurayuki suits his medium not to his own personality but to that of the woman narrator. The most obvious mannerism of her style is the repeated use of causal constructions (usually by combining the conditional and provisional inflections of verbs), although one cannot say whether Tsurayuki used such forms in a studied fashion or unconsciously as part of a simpler style.

In any event, we can see on the one hand Tsurayuki's insistence upon the spontaneous nature of song and, on the other, his use of an art so considered that it will adapt itself decorously to its subject and situation. The seeming contradiction raises the perennial question of the relation between art and life. Yet there is really no opposition in the beliefs that art makes fictional characters or stories themselves seem natural and that it is natural for man to create art. What is common to both views, and to Tsurayuki's career as we know it, is a belief in the centrality of art to life. The *Diary* itself mirrors the belief, because in a narrative about as long as a moderately short story, and in a story involving the lower nobility and other more-or-less common people of the age, there are about four hundred lines of verse. Old people and children, the middling great and the certainly humble, the courtier from the capital and the rustic of the province—"is there any living being not given to song?" Tsurayuki's faith obviously mirrors that of his society.

To him and his society poetry was a means to clarify life, sustain it, and indeed celebrate it. Although nature is often seen as a threat in the *Diary*, because of the uncertain nature of travel by sea, it is a source of great consolation to the travelers, who repeatedly pay tribute to it in their poems. What is true essentially of the poetry is true more diffusely of the prose. Both, but especially poetry, manage to create a joy that includes men and women, old and young, even past and present.

> Here are the pine trees
> That have passed through countless ages;
>   Still the breezes blow,
> Rustling through them with a voice
> Unchanged in coolness from the past.

With the theme of the centrality of art and of its ability to celebrate the richness of life goes another, tragic theme. The narrative has woven through it the dark thread of a mother's grief for her lost child. The theme is treated with equal delicacy and force. When (II. 4) she sees little shells and pretty pebbles on the shore, the mother thinks at once of her child, who would have played with them. It is a very natural image of children's play, and to have it imagined by the mother shows how much she understands just what it is she has lost; the episode is one that speaks to every parent's heart. Or again, as they pass Sumiyoshi (II. 5), the woman thinks of the famous "grasses of forgetfulness" growing there and longs to try them. Her reason cannot be bettered: "My intention was not that I should utterly forget, but that just for a moment I might

rest my aching heart and then return with renewed
strength for loving" her girl. Even in her joy at reaching
home, the mother thinks of the child she has lost, keeping in her heart her own overpowering grief and in her
diary alone the poems she writes about her child. The
woman emerges as a person of great sensibility and discrimination, rent by a tragedy but too well mannered to
exhibit her grief to others.

There is a question as to how far the tragedy dominates
the *Diary*. There are as well humor, joy, and celebration of
life. Such mingling of tones is not just a characteristic of
much Japanese literature; it is also true to human experience that life is compounded of many moods. No one, not
even a suffering mother, can devote herself completely to
her sorrow. It is as though the dark tragic thread is en-
twined by a bright one of joy in this world. All the same,
it is the darker meaning that constitutes the deeper theme
of the *Diary*. The whole, or nearly the whole, is presented
through the consciousness of the woman who suffers. Her
loss is not the only feature of her experience that is dealt
with, but it is the most significant. Moreover, what is true
of her is, by extension, true of her fellow passengers and
of mankind generally. The songs of the boatmen or the
talk of anguish of parting variously demonstrate the sad
human lot. More than that, the central, although wholly
implicit, metaphor for life in the *Diary* is the journey. That
metaphor is of course as familiar in other literatures as in
Japanese. What is particularly Japanese in the treatment
of it is that it is used, from this *Diary* throughout classical
literature, to convey man's joy in beauty and his sorrow
in hardship and death. At the center of the *Diary* there
stands a woman who has had to leave the capital, who
has lost her beloved daughter in the province, and who
again risks her life in the dangerous journey back to the
capital, where her house is in near ruin and her thoughts
center on her child. For the other passengers as well as
herself there are pirates to worry about, angry deities to
propitiate, storms and other threats to survive. There are
also lovely sights on the way. To put the theme very

simply, man's lot is on balance tragic in a world on balance beautiful. The dual theme is the central one of classical Japanese literature, and although it had been developed earlier in poetry, its wellspring in prose fiction is this *Diary.* Subsequent writers of diary fiction were to find ways to use a richer style, to include poems of higher quality, to deepen psychological portrayal, and to treat subjects in more resonant ways. But there could not be within the diary form any steps taken as original as Tsurayuki's in devising the form and with it a narrative point of view so sophisticated. Subsequent diaries, along with much of prose fiction in other forms, in a very real sense take as their aim the writing large of the formal possibilities and the human themes of *The Tosa Diary.*

The Diary of Izumi Shikibu

Tsurayuki had returned from Tosa in 935. In 1003 Izumi Shikibu entered into an affair with a prince of the blood, Atsumichi. As the journey had been the subject of the earlier diary, the love affair is that of the later. Instead of a representative tragedy of maternal love, we have a depiction of the psychology and romance of courtly love. So much is clear at once, but for many other features of *The Diary of Izumi Shikibu* there is more inference and speculation than there is clear evidence. The two chief problems are those of authorship and of the actual life of Izumi Shikibu.

In brief, the history of theories of authorship divides into four stages: before 1233, no known ascription of authorship; 1233 and following, the traditional ascription to Izumi Shikibu with the mention by Fujiwara Teika in his *Meigetsuki* (1233) of the *Diary* as *Izumi Shikibu*; the hypothesis, first advanced in 1934, that the work was not by Izumi Shikibu but by some other, later writer (how much later varying according to different versions of the hypothesis); and the general return, since the Pacific War, to belief in the traditional ascription of authorship to Izu-

mi Shikibu.[24] So far has reaction swung from the belief
that someone other than Izumi Shikibu composed it that
a responsible scholar could write flatly in 1965: *"The Izumi Shikibu Diary is a love diary written by Izumi Shikibu
from her own experience."*[25] The only other named person
to have been proposed as author has been Fujiwara Shunzei (1114–1204), a distinguished poet and critic who died
just two centuries after Izumi Shikibu's affair with Prince
Atsumichi. The theory of Shunzei's authorship rests almost
entirely upon one somewhat ambiguous piece of evidence
and so has few proponents today. Those who hold for some
other, unspecified authorship have a much better case. The
Diary is not mentioned, at least not unambiguously, until
about a century and a half after Prince Atsumichi's death,
and none of the poems in it appears in any imperial collection before the *Senzaishū* (*ca.* 1188), which was compiled,
it must be said, by Shunzei. Numerous other bits of evidence, none conclusive, have been produced. It is most
prudent to conclude that there are some good reasons for
doubt, and not enough reasons for certainty, that Izumi
Shikibu is the author; but that no one else is known who
is as likely to be the author. By strict rules of literary evidence, her authorship is unproven, but it seems most convenient to follow Japanese scholars and take it as a working hypothesis that the author is Izumi Shikibu until
stronger evidence against the ascription is uncovered.

Unfortunately, the details of her life are themselves obscure. It is not known when she was born or when she
died, although from 1033 she is no longer mentioned in
records of poetry-matches and similar functions at which
she might have been expected to appear. Her parentage
has been debated and her "name" is not, properly speaking, a name at all. The "Shikibu" refers to a lesser court
office, and the "Izumi" comes from the fact that her first

---

[24] The factual background of my account is most indebted to Tamai,
Nikki Bungaku no Kenkyū, and Endō Yoshimoto, *Tosa Nikki*, etc. (Tokyo,
1957).

[25] Tamai, *Nikki Bungaku no Kenkyū*, p. 152. Yoshida Kōichi is equally
positive in his *Izumi Shikibu Kenkyū* (Tokyo, 1964). In his excellent
Zenkō Izumi Shikibu Nikki, Suzuki Kazuo argues more quietly for Izumi
Shikibu's authorship. See the Bibliographical Note.

husband, Tachibana Michisada, was governor of Izumi
Province in 999, about the time of their marriage. It is
thought that the marriage lasted till 1004, but that it had
been a purely formal relation for some considerable portion of that time. In fact, it appears that it may have been
in the year of her marriage to Michisada that she entered
into the first of the two great affairs of her life, that with
Prince Tametaka, son of the cloistered Emperor Reizei
(r. 967–969). It was not surprising in terms of the mores
of his society that as an imperial prince Tametaka should
establish relations outside marriage. But he was criticized
for his going too far, addicting himself to pleasure, and not
only with Izumi Shikibu. He died in his twenty-sixth year
in 1002. It is thoughts of the broken dream of love with
Tametaka that occupy the Lady's mind at the opening of
the *Diary*.

What one is strongly inclined to call the plot is, however,
concerned with the second grand affair of Izumi Shikibu's
life, that with Tametaka's younger brother, Atsumichi, who
had entered into relations with her by the following spring
(1003). It is the vicissitudes of that relation that comprise
the basis of the *Diary*. The historical Atsumichi had a mad
first consort,[26] who does not enter the *Diary*, and after her
a second, of very high birth, a sister of a wife of the crown
prince. Her characterization in the *Diary* is, not very sur-
prisingly, unfavorable. She is haughty, cold, and self-im-
portant. So she may have been in reality. But even to someone not altogether strait-laced, it must have seemed highly
questionable for Prince Atsumichi to become infatuated
with a social nobody like Izumi Shikibu, who had been
mistress of his elder brother while married to Michisada.
His taking her into his palace and treating her as the most
important person there could only involve neglect of the
consort and seem a terrible affront to anyone in her position. The Lady is installed on XII. 18. The *Diary* closes
sometime after the New Year's festivities for the Prince's

---

[26] "Consort" is used to translate *"kita no kata."* On the extraordinarily
complex marriage customs of the time, see William McCullough, "Japanese Marriage Institutions in the Heian Period," *Harvard Journal of
Asian Studies*, XXVII (1967), 103–167.

father. Izumi Shikibu herself (distinguishing her from
the Lady of the *Diary*) led a few years of brilliant if questionable life thereafter, perhaps the most famous and illuminating episode in her affair being her attendance at
the Kamo Festival in 1005. Atsumichi took her in his carriage, flaunting her in the public eye by having her gor-
geous robes drape out the back, and causing her to be the
scandalous cynosure of the festival. When he died in 1007,
he was in his twenty-seventh year, Izumi Shikibu perhaps
somewhat older.

Subsequent events in her life need be only briefly mentioned. In fact, the information is scanty. The next important thing known of her is her service at the very literary
court of Empress Akiko (Shōtō Mon'in, 988–1074). Arthur
Waley's well-known comparison of Akiko to Queen Victoria[27] is quite misleading. Victoria did not gather about
her four of the most brilliant women writers of the day—
including the woman supposed the country's greatest nov-
elist and the century's finest poet. She did not learn boxing
which, Waley so amusingly says, is the Victorian equivalent of Akiko's study of masculine Chinese with Murasaki
Shikibu. And certainly only a fervid imagination could picture Victoria admitting to her service a woman with the
scandalous reputation of Izumi Shikibu. Victoria benefits
too much by the comparison, and Akiko's court was—as
far as one can judge—assembled for the brilliance of its
ladies. The best description of the group is that of Murasaki
Shikibu (*ca.* 978–*ca.* 1016) in her *Diary*. The traditionally
ascribed author of *The Tale of Genji* and a poet of some
merit, Murasaki Shikibu was also inclined to be severe
upon such weaker sisters as Sei Shōnagon and Izumi Shikibu. "How interestingly Izumi Shikibu writes!" she says,
adding, "Yet what a disgraceful [*keshikaranu*] person she
is!"[28] That is fair enough, but when she adds that Izumi

---

27 Waley (trans.), *The Tale of Genji*, p. xvi.
28 Ikeda Kitan, *et al.* (eds.), *Makura no Sōshi, Murasaki Shikibu Nikki*
(Tokyo, 1958; *Nihon Koten Bungaku Taikei*). The passage has been
somewhat variously interpreted; a frequent glossing of the first sentence
interprets it as a reference to writing letters. As for the second sentence,
Tamai in his *Murasaki Shikibu Nikki* (Tokyo, 1952; *Nihon Koten Zensho*)
glosses my "disgraceful" as "abandoned," "profligate."

Shikibu "could not practice the true art of poetry," she has gone too far, allowing her moral judgment to become entangled with her poetic rivalry.

While catching the sharp eyes of Murasaki Shikibu, she seems also to have engaged the attention of Fujiwara Yasumasa (958–1036), a man closer to her own rank than the two princes had been. Yasumasa and she were married, and she accompanied him on at least one of his posts as provincial administrator. Whether the second marriage was much more successful than the first is not known, though it may be doubted. At all events, five or six named lovers apart from those mentioned in this account appear in headnotes to her poems, and that there were yet others seems to be implied. From all such connections, she had but one known child, Koshikibu, to whom she devoted a considerable share of her seemingly inexhaustible capacity for love. Koshikibu herself was something of a poet and lover like her mother, but she died in childbirth in 1025. Izumi Shikibu's poems show that she also had strong affections for her family, which was embarrassed by her reputation. They also show that she felt shame for the scandal she caused and that, for all her worldliness, she was genuinely drawn to religion.

It is just such intensity and complexity in her character that makes the *Diary* so interesting. It is obvious that she was a passionate woman. At one point the *Diary* says of the Lady that when she looked on the Prince, "It even felt as if her very eyes grew amorous," and amorous eyes Izumi Shikibu certainly had. It is equally plain that she exercised an irresistible fascination on numerous men. The interest she held for them may be partly explained by her reputation. If Prince Tametaka had devoted himself to her, a lesser man might find some interest. Partly it may have been her appearance. At least the Prince is smitten when he finds the Lady slighter, younger looking than he had expected, and it may well have been the case that she seemed younger than she was or than her clever mind suggested. Even together, however, these two explanations are far from sufficient. She had first to earn the reputation. And the Prince does not get to see what the Lady really looks like until months after he has spent nights with her, and it is in fact an embarrassment to her, as it would have been to any noblewoman, to be seen by daylight, publicly. Apart from a passionate receptivity, what really made her attractive was her expressiveness, her sensitivity, and her mystery. Even Murasaki Shikibu had to allow that she was "interesting" and "beguiling" (*okashiki*).

The Lady's sensitivity to nature and human moods is most obviously revealed in her poems and in her long pensée written at dawn after the Prince has knocked at her door (pp. 121–122, below). The same evidence shows her expressiveness. It is significant that a poem, an observant remark, or some other cultivated gesture repeatedly brings the Prince round when his attentions have wandered from her. It is not beauty, certainly not anything material to be gained from her, but a depth and force of personality that constitute her appeal. Like all great sirens, she has an inner realm of mystery. It is this that the reader comes imperceptibly to feel, and the differing nature of her mysterious attractions from those of Helen or Cleopatra can be judged by a scene when the Prince is visiting her.

He looked upon her lying there in the bone-chilling cold, rapt in her thoughts. Many people spoke ill of her, but when she lay here before him like this, his heart stirred with love. In such a state of aroused feelings, he watched her relaxed posture, half in thought and half-asleep. Touching her gently, he whispered,

> There is no drizzle,
> There is no dew that falls tonight,
>   But as we lie here,
> A strange wetness glistens softly
> Upon the sleeve of the pillowing arm.

She did not reply, as she lay there in the languor of thought. Only, he could see the tears falling from her eyes and sparkling in the moonlight. Looking upon her with the utmost tenderness he said, "Why don't you reply? I know that what I said was unimportant—I must have said something wrong."

"What should I say?" she asked. "My thoughts are lost in a maze of feeling, and your words have scarcely entered my ears. But this much I hope you believe—your poem about 'the sleeve of the pillowing arm' is one I will never forget. You may put me to the test on *that.*" She spoke this with a sudden smile.

Her pensive withdrawal arouses his passion—it is the only time in the *Diary* that he is said to touch her—and, significantly, also leads him to a poem. She responds at once with tears—and at last with sudden humor.

That complexity, that charm, that inscrutability make the Lady of the *Diary* a very effective character. However like or unlike Izumi Shikibu the characterization is, whatever the authorship of the work, it is art rather than autobiography. It may well be that some people would wish, with Murasaki Shikibu, to censure the life of Izumi Shikibu, but the Lady of the *Diary* (she is never referred to by any name) is a fictional creation of great interest. The nature of the interest may be described in a word—romance.[29] What that romance means to a Japanese can best be represented by a phrase in the Prince's poem just quoted: "the sleeve of the pillowing arm" (*Tamakura no sode*). The image evoked is of courtly lovers in a shadowy villa, lying together on or under their robes, pillowing themselves in each other's arms. It is the image of full joy and full communion, the realization of desire—but revealed dimly by the beams of a clouded moon, leaving what is seen to suggest the preciousness of all that is hidden. It moves to tears and it allows humor. It is the Japanese version of Troilus's night with Criseyde or Porphyro's with Madeline.

The aura of romance is accompanied by an equally significant element, the psychological revelation—delineation is too crude—of the Lady and the Prince. Their personalities emerge from ebbs, flows, and halts of action, and they are made up of a tracery of moods and motives. Two things deserve emphasis, however, for their importance in the revelation of the Lady. The first is a major feature of the *Diary* until that unfortunate break near the end when she moves to the palace; until then her consciousness domi-

---

[29] See *Introduction to Classical Japanese Literature*, produced by the Kokusai Bunka Shinkōkai (Tokyo, 1948, 1956), p. 83.

nates the *Diary* by vibrating between her inner world with its own rhythm and the outer world in its passage of time. The beat is like that of Japanese music, always inevitable but often unexpected. The other element is an inner drama poised against the explicit plot of her relationship with the Prince. She is divided in her mind in longing for the security, the opportunity to love, and the triumph that living in the Prince's palace would bring, and in fearing to commit herself to what will be thought scandalous (her family is shown to be against it), and also in fearing a loss of power over her own little world, a loss of freedom to lie, however unhappily, in the shadows of her own room. Set against the problem of the Prince's likelihood of commitment to her is, therefore, the additional problem of whether she will commit herself to him. It is this withholding, like the withdrawal into her own thoughts that night of the sleeve of the pillowing arm, that is so certainly feminine and an important basis for her appeal. There is no ladder-like series of steps to a single destination in this story, because it is the essence of the experience that it ebbs and flows, that it plays off an inner and an outer plot as well as human variability against the steady forward progress of time.

It must be admitted that the ending loses such qualities. Once the story shifts to the palace, we lose any immediacy with the Prince, much less the Lady. Significantly, there are no poems in this section, and instead of either psychological truth or romance, we get a happy ending and, to put the best face on it, a kind of social realism describing what happens when a Prince establishes a favorite in his palace. The subject has some interest in its own right, but it is not relevant to what precedes it in the *Diary*. The failure reveals the extent to which the central interest of the work is the consciousness of the Lady and, to a lesser extent, of the Prince. When we move out of that realm, all turns false, as the postscript to the *Diary* seems to recognize.[30]

---

[30] See the conclusion of n. 79 to the *Diary*; other interpretations of the postscript are given there. Suzuki comments on the unsatisfactory character of the ending (*Zenkō Izumi Shikibu Nikki*, pp. 358–362). He thinks the move to the Prince's palace required a shift to omniscient authorship and that the author, finding the new technique ill suited with the old, decided at last to end the work.

Until that point the *Diary* very skillfully employs a shifting narrative point of view that is unique in the diaries of the time and very unusual by Western standards.[31] The method involves entering into the thoughts of the Lady and the Prince alike and also moving out of them to an omniscient narration. The absence of the equivalent of English personal pronouns enables this technique to function without strain or artifice. As often in classical Japanese fiction, it is also often not clear whether a given phrase is spoken, indirectly quoted, or thought. Such handlings create a general authorial omniscience, but one with very little tyranny, very little distance from the characters, and within it an entry into a consciousness dominating a given passage. Usually that is the Lady's, but it may be the Prince's. In one notable instance a very long sentence accommodates four alternating consciousnesses: the Prince's and the Lady's, each of which is expressed once in speech and once in thought. The emphasis upon the Lady is so strong most of the time that it would not be far wrong to use the first person in translation. The emphasis is revealed by the honorifics employed for the Prince and the more level language used for her, as well as by the occasional application to her of words like *konata*, which may mean "here," "this person," or even "I." Yet this closeness to her consciousness, which so skillfully allows the revelation of personality in the story, has at the same time an esthetic distance, a separation by what amounts to a basically third-person narration in the shifts away from her viewpoint to that of the Prince or general omniscience. So various and combined a method is not easily rendered, but what has been attempted in this translation is a kind of indirect quotation (as well as direct) or attribution of thought like that used on occasion by English novelists as late as Jane Austen, a more explicit or less involved stream of consciousness.

The faulty ending shows that *The Diary of Izumi Shikibu* triumphs in the revelation of the world of private experience. The Lady's child and her family are only fleetingly

---

[31] The absence of such a shifting viewpoint in other works of the time is a reason given by those who suggest later authorship. But of course a technique has to be innovated sometime.

hinted at, and the rest of society or of the public world is ignored. The "world" (*yo no naka*) which is introduced in the first sentence is that of love, and the operative word is "dream." As the central metaphor for Japanese courtly love, dream helps convey the romantic atmosphere of the story. Yet there is more to it than that. The dream had been reality till Prince Tametaka's death, and the new world of love with Prince Atsumichi is sure equally to evolve into a dream. The experience is dreamlike in the thematic sense of the illusion of temporal matters in Buddhist belief. If the Lady "yields to karma" in deciding finally to go to the Prince's palace, that too is part of the dream, because although one has no power over one's karma, she freely yields to it because she has at last convinced herself that she should go to him. Such complexity of motivation in such an atmosphere is essential to the enduring appeal of the *Diary*. Whether or not it was written by Izumi Shikibu herself, there is no doubt that it simplifies and in a sense purifies her life by defining it into a single rich episode and by rendering fact into fiction. That very fiction, while transforming a questionable life into unquestionable art, maintains forever alive the human attraction of a woman who died over nine centuries ago.

The Narrow Road Through the Provinces

It was late in 1003 when Izumi Shikibu was taken to Prince Atsumichi's palace. It was the spring of 1689 when Matsuo Bashō (1644–1694) left Edo on a journey that was to last more than two and a half years, the first six months of which are related in *The Narrow Road Through the Provinces*. Much had changed in seven centuries. The capital remained at what we call Kyoto, but it was Bashō's Edo, the thriving ancestor of a yet more thriving Tokyo, and the Osaka of the dramatist Chikamatsu that possessed social and literary vitality. In a series of bloody wars power had passed from courtiers and warriors within the court society to a warrior aristocracy with its own constitution of society. By the seventeenth century there were signs of growing

mercantile power. Instead of the courtly distinction between the "good" people—the nobility—and the unconsid-
ered majority, there was now a division into four feudal
classes (see n. 10 to *The Narrow Road*) and with it numerous laws that in theory at least kept rigid social distinctions. In the realm of writing itself, the language of prose
had simplified somewhat in inflections and more markedly
in syntax, and it had been enriched, or at least swelled, by
Chinese borrowings which increased its potential for ab-
straction and its range of specification. There are many reflections of such changes in Bashō's diary. Repeated references to great military figures or an occasional comment on
a merchant reflect the social changes.[32] The alteration in
style and language is self-evident in the original, although
translation cannot convey the shift from a purely Japanese
medium to Bashō's denser mixture with words derived from
Chinese. But the best symbol of change can be glimpsed in
the figure of Bashō walking off towards the obscure northern and western regions of Japan. (See figs. 14 and 15.)
The greatest poet of the Tokugawa period is a restless
priest of relatively humble origins in the military aristocracy, setting off on foot at forty-five years of age, in this one
journey using half of the remainder of his life and in a
frame of mind half expecting to die.

That priestly figure is one that had been self-impelled
from an early age by an urge to poetry and discovery. Born
in Iga Province in 1644, he studied (some think) under the
distinguished scholar and poet of linked verse, Kitamura
Kigin (1624–1705) and had two poems published by 1664.
About 1666 he ran off to the capital, where he lived until
1671, studying Japanese classics, Chinese classics, and cal-
ligraphy under three of the best teachers of the day. It must
have been life he studied in the person of one Juteini, who
was his mistress during these years. After a brief return
home, he set out to Edo and there studied with an Edo disciple of the Osaka poet, Nishiyama Sōin (1605–82), and
gradually defined his own styles, collecting disciples and

---

[32] See, for example, nn. 15, 52, and 54 to the translation and the
passages they gloss.

patrons as he met with increasing acclaim. Yet by 1684 he began his years of impatient wayfaring. He had traveled here and there before, but with the purpose of getting away from some place or to some destination. Now he was traveling for the sake of the journey, for being in movement. A short journey in 1687 was followed by a long one begun the same year. He was back at the end of the year and off again in two months to Suma and Sarashina. As he says at the opening of *The Narrow Road*, he came home from Sarashina to dust out cobwebs, to dispose of his "doll's house," and go off again.

The personality of Bashō and the changes in society since the eleventh century led inevitably to changes in the conception and execution of the poetic diary. Along with the new prose medium there is a new poetic form, the two elements combining to create a form of expression of experience differing in many respects from those of *The Tosa Diary* or *The Diary of Izumi Shikibu*. The formal nature of Bashō's *haikai* has already been discussed. It need only be added that the fact that his poems are conceived of as potential "opening stanzas" (*hokku*) for continuation in longer *haikai* units can be shown by the fact that a number of poems in *The Narrow Road* were so used by Bashō and others gathering together at this or that place on his travel. The sense of something else to be added in *haikai* both increases the adherence of the poem to its prose context and provides high moments of style, reverberations subsiding once again into the more even temper of the prose.

It was inevitable that six centuries should produce major changes in society and in literary media. And it was necessary that Bashō should have some manner of distinctive personality if his works were to achieve a special greatness. And yet one can go too far in regarding him wholly as a Tokugawa poet in the company of the brilliant but less profound Ihara Saikaku (1642–1693) and the gifted dramatist Chikamatsu. The danger is that he may be taken out of the tradition in which he was writing. He himself saw that he was writing poetic diaries as one of a long line of writers, and also that he was so much within a tradition that the problem was to make his efforts original. In his *Essay from a Traveller's Bookcase*,[33] he wrote:

> To begin with, diaries of the road were written by Ki no Tsurayuki, Kamo no Chōmei, and the Nun Abutsu. They wrote excellent works, but since them all other writers have merely tried to recapture what had been done before, and so have not been able to create anything new from the dregs of the past.[34]

It is of considerable interest that Bashō thinks of his travel records as diaries and that he should set *The Diary of the Waning Moon* as the last work of the form to be really creative, since he thereby suggests not only that he will seek a new departure in order to create a living form, but also that the only great diaries belong to the courtly past. Nothing between about 1280 and his own day was (avowedly, at least) of crucial use to him, and yet different as he might be, Tsurayuki remained an inspiration.

There is a good deal of evidence besides to show that Bashō was indebted to the courtly past. It is a striking fact, for example, that in *The Narrow Road* Bashō alludes repeatedly to court poets but not at all to earlier *haikai* poets. What is new is not a turning back on his inheritance, because he deeply prized it. What is new is his artistic search, not for the high esthetic beauty as such that the court poets prized in one fashion or another, but a beauty that admitted the "low" (*zoku*).[35] Some court poets, notably Priest Saigyō (1118–1190) had taken steps in the direction of the humble, and Bashō is given to alluding to their poems. But he goes the whole distance, while yet retaining enough of the courtly sense to keep old images or to give a poetic

---

[33] The Japanese title is *Oi no Kobumi*. Significantly, the work is also called *Oi Nikki* (*Diary of a Traveller's Bookcase*), as well as by other names.

[34] *Oi no Kobumi* in Sugiura Shōichirō, *et al.* (eds.), *Bashō Bunshū* (Tokyo, 1959; *Nihon Koten Bungaku Taikei*), p. 53. The mention of Chōmei (d. 1216) involves a then falsely attributed work.

[35] Bashō's debt to the courtly past and his alteration of it by use of the "low" and by other emphases are points made by Professor Konishi, *Nihon Bungakushi* (Tokyo, 1953), pp. 108–11. In his "Bashō to Heian Bungei," *Bashō Kōza* (Tokyo, 1956), IV, he stresses Bashō's debt to Heian diaries and the fact that his travel diaries are highly artistic works, not mere travel records.

status to such images as toads, fleas, and lice. Another important development, aided by some hints in *The Tosa Diary*, is Bashō's creation of a tension between the forward movement of the travel diary in space and time and the importance of individual and therefore static stages. The forward element is perfectly evident in the tone of restlessness throughout the work and in the conclusion, which shows Bashō impelled yet farther on, as if on a new and yet unending journey. The coherence and fixed importance of individual episodes will be most readily understood by the prose poems on Matsushima, Hiraizumi, and Kisa Bay. But there are other symptoms—the use of military imagery to unify the Kurobane episode and allusion to the "Yūgao" chapter of *The Tale of Genji* to lend coherence to the Fukui episode. The "low" images in the latter are set against one of the most beautiful of court stories, and Bashō's achievement can only be understood by recognizing the association and the contrast together.

There is no widely accepted view about the structure of *The Narrow Road Through the Provinces*, none that is at once comprehensive and detailed. One view advanced recently is that the episodes are arranged in a complex parallelism and an almost complete circle beginning in Edo and ending in Ōgaki. Bashō's own explicit comparison between Matsushima and Kisa Bay lends some credence to the interpretation, but *haikai* poets deliberately avoided such structures. If we consider the two barrier episodes—at Shirakawa Barrier and Ichiburi Barrier—we find little further resemblance. An altogether more likely possibility is that Bashō adapts the structure of a *haikai* sequence. The elevated opening corresponds to the *hokku*, or opening verse, of a *haikai*, and most of Bashō's changes from fact as recorded in Sora's *Diary* or his introduction of fictionalized episodes can be understood as an attempt to follow the poetic pattern. In a proper *haikai*, for example, there was a requirement for one love-verse (*koi no ku*) in one of several certain places. Bashō's story of the encounter with prostitutes at Ichiburi is thought wholly fictional by most scholars. Significantly, it comes at a juncture appropriate for a love verse. There is no question but that the whole diary has the feel of *haikai*, as perhaps the poems make inevitable, and we may hope for detailed analysis along such lines.[36] Of course the diary remains an artistic version of a certain journey, but the effect of considered art is so strong that a close reading suggests, if it does not wholly uncover, a closely ordered structure.

Most readers have been content to set to one side the means by which Bashō achieves his effects and to interest themselves in the effects alone—the experience developed in *The Narrow Road*. It lacks the originality and human normality of *The Tosa Diary*, as well as the romance and psychology of *The Diary of Izumi Shikibu*. But it is a greater work than either, partly because of the very high order of some of the poetry, partly because it admits a wider variety of experience, and partly because of the deep significance it discovers in the experience. Something will be said about the poems in a later section of this Introduction. Something has been said already about the variety and coherence of the work, but to convey the way in which the diversity is given depth one must consider its inner relations. There is the past. Allusions to the Chinese classics, recollections of court poems and legends, attention to native religion, repeated concern with native chivalric stories —each of these differs from the others but all suggest high motifs in an inheritance from the past. There is also the present. The most immediate aspect of the work is that which Bashō encounters, the sights of travel, the people met. The sights include the grandeur of Matsushima (upon which Bashō refuses to write a poem), the filth of Iizuka, the lodgings with prostitutes at Ichiburi, and the irritating young priests at Daijōji. The interplay between that past and present accounts for much of the rich coloring of Bashō's world.

The depth of experience he discovers in the mingled past and present can be understood in terms of his attitudes. The past is more romantic than the present, but it is also more tragic—as the magnificent Hiraizumi episode shows—be-

---

[36] The parallel theory is advanced by Nobuyuki Yuasa in the Introduction to his useful translation, *The Narrow Road to the Deep North and Other Travel Sketches*, Penguin Books, 1966, p. 38. The *haikai* reading is that of Professor Konishi in a letter to me; I have but sketched some of the details.

FIG. 4. Masaoka Shiki as a Young Man
From Shiki Zenshū.

Courtesy of Kadokawa Shoten

FIG. 5. A Leaf from *The Tosa Diary*

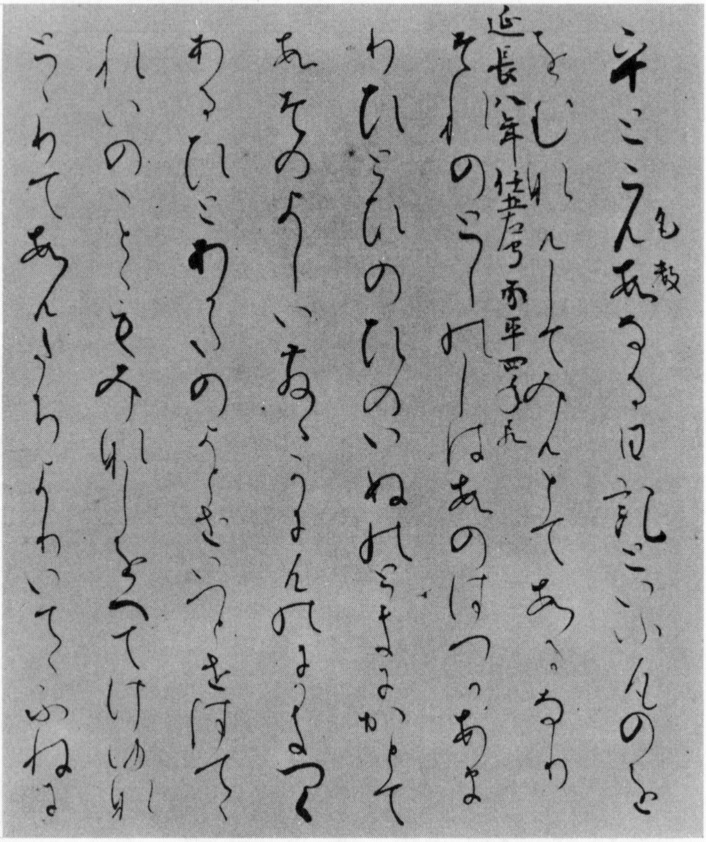

cause it reveals the tragic waste of time. The present is far
more variable and often is lacking in appeal, but it is certainly more immediate. And it is often very revealing. Suffering from the effects of a leaking ceiling, fleas, and lice at
Iizuka, Bashō has an attack from an old malady. When he
is well received, the affliction goes away. Or again, the irritation with young priests who pester the great poet from
Edo for some verses is due in considerable measure to
Bashō's being out of sorts from Sora's having left him. He
obviously knew that such details revealed his warts and
bumps. And yet he includes them. In other words, the reve-
lations and encounters of the present, like the resonances
from the past, give the reader a greater interest in Bashō
himself than in his journey, and it is highly likely that his
account of it in *The Narrow Road* was for him, as it is for
us, a means of understanding his complex personality. It is
not indeed his weaknesses that make him appear the less a
saint, because their nature only gives credibility to a picture of a good man. What does seem less saintly, though
much more interesting, is the great complexity of his personality. He is aware of so much—his memory and imagination swell with associations from the past—and his rapid
movements of mind and heart from the high or sublime to
the low reveal a very wide-eyed, knowing man.

And yet neither the past and the present together nor the
many-faceted, observant personality suffice to account for
the power of *The Narrow Road*, a force driving on its cre-
ator as well as the style and meaning of the work. The
source of that drive can be understood by comparison with
The Tosa Diary. There, the journey was necessary for getting home, and the destination was dearly hoped for. With
Bashō, the journey is in a sense without a destination, or is
all destination, since he has disposed of his house before
leaving. If Tsurayuki implicitly creates the journey as a
metaphor for life, Bashō was obsessed with the idea, as the
opening of *The Narrow Road* shows. Probably not even a
Japanese could explain Bashō's motives in their fullness,
but several matters do appear to be involved in his insatiable urge to travel. There is one simple one that must not be
forgot—the desire to visit places he had not seen. Another
kind of motive is his preoccupation with time, which

arouses a restlessness in him. Yet another is the tradition of wandering priests. Bashō is involved in a search of past and present, of places, people, and ideas. The past and the present are caught up in the flux of the journey, and with them is entangled the future with its implications of death. Japanese attitudes toward death differ from Western, but if we understand *The Narrow Road* as a subtler treatment of Tennyson's theme in "Ulysses"—of the compulsion to know life most fully, even including death—we shall not be far wide of the mark. With Bashō, religious vocation, psychological promptings, and literary interests combine to create a view of life at once moving and somewhat disturbing in its restlessness.

Events of the last five years of his life convey aspects of his personality very forcibly. For the first half of the period, he continued on the journey described in *The Narrow Road*. In the winter of 1691 he returned to Edo and sought to immure himself from the world. For this action (as well as for his compulsive wandering) there are numerous explanations, including the religious and the psychological, as one knows from seeing Bashō's actions relived by the lives of one's Japanese friends. But Bashō could not remain silent. He might bar the door of his house, as it were, but he could not close the door of his heart. Between 1691 and 1693 he produced two collections of poems. And as the spring of 1694 came, Bashō could stay put no longer and set off on his last journey. He had gone before on the usual routes and even to the relatively unknown north and west. Now he was driven to go to the southern tip of Japan. He got no farther than the Osaka area, where he fell ill and knew himself that his longest journey was at last coming to an end. On X. 8, four days before he died, he showed that a whirl of past and present, time and eternity, illusion and reality still turned about in his head. About midnight he produced his last great poem.

> Stricken in travel—
> And over withered moors my dreams
> Turn about and about.

As the openings of works as various as *The Diary of Izumi Shikibu* or *The Tale of the Heike* show, the image of dream is one of the most powerful in Japanese literature. Bashō himself had had to sit down and weep at Hiraizumi and its "vestiges of a dream." Even in 1694 illusions and visions, specters and bright shapes moved in his mind as he lay dying.

Most people find on their first reading of *The Narrow Road* that its middle sections are the most interesting. Our initial reactions are of considerable literary as well as personal value, but so are our subsequent responses, and these show the appeal of the beginning and ending as well. Certainly it is true that the meaning of the work, like the personality of its author, can be understood only by encompassing in the mind the total work in its variety. Or perhaps that is wrong, because in another sense the only way to understand the experience treated is, so to speak, to undergo it oneself, yielding to each place or event or encounter as it comes along. Or, finally, what we should seek to do is *both* yield like Bashō to the way and seek to understand the whole. Such an effort may be vain, the aim impossible for the reader. But it is the effort motivating Bashō, giving a special power to *The Narrow Road Through the Provinces*, and evoking a moving response in the reader.

The Verse Record of My Peonies

Some three centuries after Bashō lay "Stricken in travel," Masaoka Shiki (1867–1902) was suffering one of his agonizing experiences of being bedridden with a particularly painful form of spinal tuberculosis. When on that day in May, 1899 two friends brought him a pot of peonies, he used them as a focus for a brief diary of his affliction. In the three hundred years between, there had come about fundamental social and literary changes. The change is most simply described as one from government by a military aristocracy to something approaching constitutional monarchy in the nation and from richness to realism in literature. There had been a strong element of the "low" in Bashō's writing, but that had been harmonized with the

high and grand. Shiki set about to emphasize the ordinary
by formulating an ideal of descriptive realism (*shasei*),
which allows in his diary for talk of medicine, enemas, and
thermometers as well as for recollections of Bashō.

Shiki is the most effective kind of literary revolutionary
—he who is deeply committed to the past but insists that
it has been misunderstood. He was a noted *tanka* poet—
the form used by Tsurayuki and the court—as well as the
greatest *haiku* poet of his time, but he reacted strongly
against Tsurayuki's prestige and all that it symbolized. He
almost denied that Tsurayuki was a poet at all. Shiki's alteration of the topography of Japanese poetry still seems
the proper description to many Japanese who find the
Man'yōshū true and great, the *Kokinshū* and Tsurayuki
artificial. Shiki was less successful in arguing that the
haikai poét Yosa (or Taniguchi) Buson (1716–1784) possessed greater merit than Bashō, but his belief tells something about his own ideal of descriptive realism, since
Buson, perhaps from his experience as a painter, excels in a
delineation at once clear and sensuous. Such new views
about the past were accompanied by a change in poetic
medium. Shiki is properly styled a *haiku* poet, as Bashō is
a *haikai* poet. By the late nineteenth century the form of
5–7–5 syllables had grown explicitly autonomous; it was no
longer an initial or any other unit in a formal sequence, pu-
tative or actual. The new autonomy does not, however, prevent Shiki from integrating his *haiku* with prose or from
writing what often appear to be *haiku* variations on a
theme.

His realism, wry humor, and force of mind are very
quickly felt in this brief *Verse Record*. Beyond such qualities, the meaning of the work involves the symbolism of the
peonies. He initially draws a contrast between himself in
his "hell of fire," and the flowers with their name, "Thin
Ice." Their beauty represents the attractiveness of the lovely exterior world in contrast with his personal agony. Yet it
is not long before the peonies come to symbolize his illness
and uncertain future. They, too, are in the power of others
and of time. As the last poem shows, the brief life of the
flowers is what defines for Shiki the nature of his three

days, what gives the *Verse Record* its unity. The symbolism suggests a certain feverishness of observation which is altogether natural under the circumstances. Shiki was so ill that he had to dictate one portion. And yet he retains hold on his "descriptive realism," as one of the poems most admired by his followers shows.

> Two flakes fall
> And the shape of the peonies
> Is wholly changed.

The poem inevitably recalls a *haikai* verse by Buson, one of his most famous and one commonly given to illustrate his objectivity.

> The peonies fall
> And they pile on each other,
> Two or three flakes.[37]

As the example suggests, there is a curious tendency during the most serious portion of the illness to recall the esthetic beauty and clear depiction found in Buson's poetry. The recollection of a favorite poet is not curious in itself, but it is strange when coupled with the fact that when the illness abates, the image in his mind is that of Bashō. To recall objective Buson during the feverish imaginings of the second day and then to think of the more subjective Bashō as his mind becomes more settled is to overturn one's expectations. Such a tension resembles that of the symbolism of the flowers—first as a contrast with him, then as a symbol of his illness, and at the end something of both. A similar contrast might be drawn between the ordinariness of the prose and the artistic feel—however realistic they may be—of the poems.

Many people visit Shiki during the three days and this suggests something of the loyalties he aroused and the impression he created on others. The usual photograph of him (see fig. 13) is not at all attractive, but it does convey something of his strength and it is curiously impressive. Shiki and the Meiji period also lend this book a certain fortuitous

---

[37] Poem no. 521 in Teruoka Yasutaka and Kawashima Tsuyu (eds.), *Busonshū Issashū* (Tokyo, 1959; *Nihon Koten Bungaku Taikei*).

symmetry. He was born in Matsuyama, to the north of that
Tosa Province in Shikoku from which Tsurayuki had set
out. The Tosa military were among the most influential in
promoting the Meiji Restoration and in directing the life of
the period. Many people from Tosa had in abundance that
energy, that sense of historical mission, and that capacity
for achievement that so marks the bustling Meiji era. Shiki
possessed these qualities, too, for although he is obviously
seriously ill during May, 1899—and in fact died three years
later—there is a burning Meiji vitality about him and his
writing. Such a quality, which we seldom associate with
realism, helps account for the appeal of *The Verse Record
of My Peonies* and assists in understanding Shiki, both as a
man and as the leading poet-critic of his day.

Poetry and Diaries

If we must think long before recalling any truly literary
diaries in languages other than Japanese, it is yet harder
to advance any but a Japanese diary that can be strictly
termed poetic. What is difficult in other literatures is simple in Japanese. The most recent study discusses almost
thirty literary diaries written between 935 and 1350.[38]
Whatever Bashō's opinion about the quality of what he
calls "diaries of the road" after *The Diary of the Waning
Moon*, the fact remains that this subspecies of the form
continued to be written. Shiki has a number of diaries of
illnesses. And even since the Pacific War there have been
such distinguished examples as *The Tragedy of Man* (*Nin-*

[38] Tamai, *Nikki Bungaku no Kenkyū.* See his table of contents, which
lists more than one diary for two writers. His Chronology of Diary Literature, pp. 722–25 is instructive. His Bibliography of important editions
(pp. 726–731) is also interesting. He gives the most for *The Diary of
Murasaki Shikibu* (11), a popularity no doubt explained by its connection with *The Tale of Genji;* then *The Tosa Diary* and *The Sarashina
Diary* (6 each); and then *The Diary of Izumi Shikibu* (5). In his "Chūsei
Nikki Kikō Bungaku no Ichiran," *Bungaku,* IX (Nov. 1964), Fukuda
Shūichi catalogued ninety art diaries between 1180 and 1597, although
two have been lost and three are thought spurious. Thereafter diaries of
various kinds are so numerous that no scholar has ever attempted to
compile a bibliography.

gen no Higeki) by Takamura Kōtarō (1883–1956). Such abundance implies, what is certainly the case, that other examples might have been chosen for inclusion in this book. There is much to be said for the romantic lyricism of *The Sarashina Diary*, for the acute moral vision of *The Diary of Murasaki Shikibu*, or for the self-revelation of *The Gossamer Diary*. The actual choices for the book have, however, been governed by different preferences, and although those primarily include an assessment of historical and intrinsic quality, they also include the reason that each author selected is the greatest poet of his (or her) age. The choice from among Shiki's diaries was determined by my acquaintance with it since 1947 and by its existence in three separate, although almost wholly unannotated, editions. The choices apart, the fact that each poet is the finest of his day requires that some assessment be made of the poetry in these diaries.

To assess first the quality of poems in themselves, it must be said straight off that only *The Narrow Road Through the Provinces* contains a full sample of the poet's finest work. Bashō's journey happened to correspond in time with the full flowering of his powers, and his artistic aim introduced no complications. In writing *The Tosa Diary* in the guise of a woman, Tsurayuki had had to simplify poems for her and for other ordinary people on the voyage. That in itself, though precluding the full scope of his art, is of interest, and many of the poems have all the same an intrinsic as well as a dramatic worth that is moving. The poems of *The Diary of Izumi Shikibu* are restricted to those that pass between the Lady and the Prince and are, therefore, tied to the situation. Many are highly attractive, but it will be found that they are far more meaningful within their context than without. Shiki's poems are on a level with most of his work but not really outstanding. By contrast it may be said of Bashō that five or six of the poems in *The Narrow Road Through the Provinces* would be included in any anthology of his works. And yet readers of this book will be forcibly struck by the fact that they mean incomparably more in their diary context. The poems are not only more meaningful in their contexts but also often quite different in meaning from that which emerges from their existence *in vacuo*. It is almost as if we must think of a genre of "diary poetry" to contrast with "free poetry."

What is involved is not so much an evaluative as a descriptive consideration. Everyone is familiar with the brevity of Japanese poetic forms and the ways in which what was short to begin with becomes yet shorter with the centuries. The change from *tanka* to *haikai* verses to *haiku* in the works included here illustrates that history. At the same time, there is an opposite process of integration of those shorter units. It can be seen functioning in the integration of *tanka* poems by complex methods of progression and association in anthologies and sequences; it can be found in briefer units such as the "tales of poems" (*utamonogatari*) of which *The Tales of Ise* is the most famous example; and it can be seen in various minglings of prose and verse, whether for the theater, or indeed for the diary.[39] What such various methods of integrating poems suggest is that the brief forms are considered less discrete than are Western poems. There is a presumption of relatedness, of connection between one poem and another, or between a poem and its situation of composition. No doubt without such adhesive potential, the poetic diary would never have been possible. And the integration helps account for the lack of dismay Japanese have felt as their poetic forms grew shorter: short they might be, but they were units in an unfolding larger whole. As early as the *Kokinshū*, one can read the poems on seasonal topics as a literary creation of 670 lines, and its love poems as a literary creation of 1,800 lines. Both sections include poems by various poets of different centuries, but they have been integrated by temporal progressions—of the subjects of the poems, not their authors' dates. It was with Tsurayuki and his fellow compilers of the *Ko-*

---

[39] On the integration of anthologies and sequences, see: Konishi Jin'ichi, "Association and Progression: Principles of Integration in Anthologies and Sequences of Japanese Court Poetry, A.D. 900–1350," *Harvard Journal of Asiatic Studies*, XXI (1958); also Brower and Miner, *Japanese Court Poetry*, pp. 319–329, 403–413, 491–493. The first translation of a complete sequence is that of Robert H. Brower and Earl Miner, *Fujiwara Teika's Superior Poems of Our Time* (Stanford, 1967), which includes eighty-three poems and detailed commentary on their ordering by progression and association.

kinshū that such techniques originated, although later imperial anthologies found ways for heightening the beauty of integration.

It is appropriate that the diary form, and with it prose fiction, should also begin with Tsurayuki. In some respects, the literary diary is indeed a more characteristic or peculiarly Japanese form than the anthology, because it answers to Japanese needs to know or to create the background of the poem. It really does not matter that Bashō says he entered a temple and had tea, when Sora's *Diary* makes it clear they did no such thing; or that Bashō manipulates time, changing the dates on which events occurred, as Sora's *Diary* also shows. The reader has still the feeling that Bashō's work is related to factual truth and that, therefore, the poems grow from a valid context. We are back to Chikamatsu's narrow margin between truth and fiction. And yet, even the most fictional of these diaries shows the same tendency. If it is one day proved, as is possible, that *The Diary of Izumi Shikibu* was not written by her, then the tendency would be shown in extreme form. We would have to posit some author's having taken poems from a collection of Izumi Shikibu's poetry—and perhaps making up some himself—and having woven the prose of a diary about them to give the poems their setting. Although such a proceeding is not thought likely today, it is the method that in fact produced *The Tales of Ise* (*Ise Monogatari*).

The poems of each of the diaries included here have special interests. Tsurayuki's are especially interesting for their dramatic appropriateness to a wide variety of characters. Izumi Shikibu's poems have the appeal either of being actual exchanges in that extraordinary love affair, or of having been brought together with remarkable ingenuity by a third hand to describe one of the great romances in Japanese history. A special feature of Bashō's poems is that a number of them provided the opening stanzas for *haikai* sequences composed at various places along the way. (The text shows as much, and an illustrative instance or two is recorded in the footnotes.) Such a fact shows how little cut and dried, how little tidy, Japanese forms are, since the full treatment of *The Narrow Road Through the Prov-*

inces and its poems would require somehow including at their appropriate places the sequences composed along the way. If we doubt that such inclusion is proper, we then believe that the work has a greater degree of art or fiction and esthetic distance from its author. Shiki's *haiku* have yet another tendency in their integration. The *haiku* themselves may comprise a discrete form of three lines, but he goes further than any of the other writers toward making the individual poems jewels on a string or stanzas of a sequence of poems. On May 9 there are eight poems given *seriatim*, with only one brief prose sentence (between the seventh and eighth poems) breaking the sequence. The effect is to convey almost a succession of related dream images, since the poems are governed by suggestions of fever and a statement that he "fell asleep with difficulty." The poet with the briefest, most discrete form is most given to combining single examples of it.

Each of the four diaries therefore provides a justification for what may seem a curious form, the poetic diary. And in each work the poems take on added significance by virtue of their prose or poetic settings. The mother of *The Tosa Diary* mourning her dead girl, the reverberation of the image of "the sleeve of the pillowing arm" through several poems in *The Diary of Izumi Shikibu*, Bashō weeping as he sits on his hat and writes of summer grasses at Hiraizumi, and Shiki seeing feverish images in his illness—all remain imprinted in our imaginations—and all are situations amplifying the poems. Yet it is also true that the prose is dependent upon the poetry, and that in each work the poetry is more important than the prose. The prose serves to amplify the poems much as the setting of a play serves the dialogue, or a recitative an aria. It is the poems that are the *raison d'être*, the purpose of the work, as is shown by the fact that the diary element is often only perfunctory. The absence of daily entries in two of the diaries is one symptom; the artistic transcending of the natural diary is another and more important symptom. It is the poems that bring the fullest experience of what is worthy of joy in this world or what causes human sorrow. In some of the diaries that might have been included here—*The Diary of Mura-*

saki Shikibu, for instance—there is a smaller proportion of poems, and the poems are of lower quality. The result is a greater air of fact, an approach to the side of truth on the narrow margin, although the superb prose style of Murasaki Shikibu acts in another direction to render the diary into art.

Within the diaries that follow this Introduction, there will be occasional moments when one senses a contrast in moving from poem to prose to poem, but the contrast is surely no greater than that from aria to recitative to aria, and it is usually less. One reason for such smoothness of movement between different literary modes is that the Japanese are so given, or were so given, to responding with poetry that there is a naturalness and integrity in combining the modes. Another reason is that the diary prose itself, through art, shades off from fact at one side of the narrow margin to fiction on the other side. When art is made to seem natural, or when the actual is rendered into full art, the margin becomes less important than the achievement. It is no wonder, then, that the three lengthier diaries included here are important classics or that the last, Shiki's account of three days of suffering, should have been republished by a Japanese soldier toward the close of the Pacific War. All four works are of an unusual form to those outside Japanese tradition, but in all there is sufficient human, artistic cause to render them meaningful and appealing.

The Tosa Diary
(Tosa Nikki)
by Ki no Tsurayuki

The Tosa Diary

It is said that diaries are kept by men, but I shall see if a woman cannot also keep one. It was about eight at night on the 21st of the Twelfth Month of that year[1] when we started on the trip for which I shall try to give my account. Leading our group was a certain man who had completed his four- or five-year term as chief official in that country province. He brought to an end all the usual affairs of office, and having received his certificate of replacement, he left his official residence and went down to the place where our party was to board its boat. There were many people to see us off, both those whom we knew and strangers. It is painful to part with those one has come to know over a period of years and, amid all the farewells, we found that the day had passed and night had fallen.

On the twenty-second we offered prayers to the gods that we might be able to land safely at Izumi. Fujiwara Tokizane presented us with "something for the horse," although knowing we were proceeding by ship.[2] With this the people of all ranks fell to heavy drinking, and it was surprising to see how they dissolved in their carousing by the seaside.

The 23rd.

There is a person come to us called Yagi Yasunori who does not seem to be in government service, and yet he gave our party splendid gifts. Although people do not usually come to bid farewell to a departing official, it may have been due to a good feature in the character of the governor that some of the well-disposed residents of the prov-

---

[1] It was A.D. 934 when Tsurayuki left Tosa to return to the capital. The twelfth month of the lunar calendar is January by the solar. See n. 7.

[2] Tsurayuki uses the idiomatic phrase, *uma no hanamuke*, "turning of the horse's nose," in a word play upon boat travel. The phrase recurs in the *Diary*, being used later to mean parting gifts.

ince came to our first stopping-place. So Yasunori came—
I do not praise him for his presents but for the good will
he showed.

The 24th.

The leader of a religious house came to offer parting
presents. The people present—high and low, without distinction, even the young—drank a great deal, and in the
general carousing those who could not even write a simple
line were staggering crosses with their footprints.[3]

The 25th.

A letter of invitation came from the official residence
of the new governor of the province. Our former governor
and others in his entourage went off, staying all day and
night. What with the entertainment they received, they
were there until the new day had dawned.

The 26th.

It is said that there was a great feast at the new governor's residence and that everyone, down to the least re-
tainer, was remembered with gifts. Chinese poems were
composed and recited. The host, his guest, and others also
composed Japanese poems for each other. It is not for a
woman to record the Chinese poems.[4] His Excellency the
present governor composed the following Japanese poem.

> I left the capital
> With expectations of our meeting
> And intimacy with you,
> But I find that we have had to part
> Even before a proper chance to meet.

Upon receiving the poem, our governor composed his
reply.

> White as linen,
> The waves splash back and forth together

---

[3] In Japanese the point is that those illiterates who could not draw the
single horizontal line for the number one are so drunk that their staggering
feet draw the crossed lines for ten.

[4] Women usually did not learn Chinese, though some braved social
stigma to do so. Men commonly kept diaries in Chinese, a fact related to
the first sentence of the *Diary*.

Far across the sea,
And just as I do now, you will return,
To meet me in the capital again.

There were poems composed by others, but none with any claim to style. After chatting about various matters, the two governors descended in close company to the garden where, taking each other by the hand, they talked in a convivial manner until the former governor left and the present went into his residence.

The 27th.

We set out by rowing from Ōtsu toward Urato. Amid all these things which I have related, I was filled with grief for my daughter. She had been born in the capital and had died suddenly in the province. Because of all the commotion of our departure, I have said nothing about this, but now that we are at last bound for the capital, I cannot help longing to have my dead girl alive again. The people with me wish her with us, too. I made some verses.[5]

The greatest sadness
Of thinking that now at last
We are bound for home
Is that there remains one person
Who will never know return.

And again, at another time,

I kept forgetting
That the child was dead and, asking,
As if she were alive,
"What can that girl be up to?"
I have fallen into a greater grief.

While I was reciting these verses to myself, we came to the Point of Kako, where the brothers of the new governor and many others came in a company bringing sake and other things. Our party went ashore and spoke with them

[5] The narrator can only mean she wrote the verses herself although, like many poems in the *Diary*, this is attributed to *aru hito*, "a certain person." One theory holds that all poems so designated are meant to be by Tsurayuki, the "former governor" of the *Diary*. But that confuses biography and fiction.

of the unpleasantness of parting. As they revealed in coming to us, these people are the warmest hearted among
all the people in the entourage of the new governor.

Amid this talk of unhappy farewells, our visitors brought
forth a poem together. As the proverb says, "Even a large
fishing net can be carried by many people," and so they
accompanied us down to the water's edge with an "All
together there, let's go, let's go!" and the poem.

> Regretting that you leave,
> And wondering if you might not stay,
> We come in a swarm
> Like faithful mallards among the reeds
> To hold our fellows back with us.

One of our group, being greatly affected by their poem,
composed a reply.

> So deep the ocean,
> That one may plunge in it a pole
> And not know its reaches;
> Even so great a depth of heart
> Is that which we have seen in you.

As these verses were being said, the captain of our ship,
a man lacking in warmth and far gone with sake, shouted
out, "the tide has come in—the wind will be rising, too!"
There was nothing for us to do but board the ship again.
At this, some of the people recited alongside the boat
Chinese poems appropriate to the occasion. There was
also present a certain man from the west country who
nonetheless recited some verses from songs of the eastern
provinces. Upon hearing the singing, someone praised it
highly: "With such singing, the dust on the beams of our
cabin will dance as it did for the songs of Yü Kung, and the
very clouds will linger as they did for the singing of Ch'in
Ch'ing."

We stop tonight at Urato. Fujiwara Tokizane, Tachibana
Suehira, and others of this province are following separately.

The 28th.

We rowed out from Urato, bound for Ōminato. As we were about to set out, Yamaguchi Chimine, the son of a governor in former times, brought us sake and many delicacies. We put them on the boat and enjoyed them on the way.

The 29th.

We are stopping at Ōminato. The provincial medical officer has come bringing sake and with it spiced sake and sake flavoring for New Year's celebrations. It seems to be done out of personal kindness.

New Year's Day.

We are still in the same harbor. One of our people, thinking that we had just this one night to get ready the New Year's sake flavoring, cut it up in the house erected on the deck. But the wind came in a gust, and the things fell into the sea, and we were unable to drink it after all. Since this is a province lacking such things, we have none of the special foods of the season. More than that, we are not even prepared to deal with them and have only some rather tired Tosa trout to put to our lips. What must those trout be thinking as they meet with such an affectionate gesture?

Everyone is saying, "The capital is all I can think about today. What must the small houses there look like, with the decorations of sacred rope and the mullet or holly hanging from it?"

The 2nd.

We are still harbored at Ōminato. The ecclesiastical official has presented us with foodstuffs and sake.

The 3rd.

We are still in the same place. I wonder if the wind and waves are not thinking, "We would be happy if you would stay here a little longer." The delay is very unpleasant to us all.

The 4th.

Since the wind is blowing high, we are unable to set out. Masatsura[6] has presented us with sake and other delicacies. In such circumstances as ours it is very trying always to be receiving gifts and never having anything to return but thanks. We simply have nothing proper to give, and so although we have become—ever so wealthy—we feel rather cheap.

The 5th.

Since the wind has not gone down, we remain in the same place. The local people have been unfailing in their visits.

The 6th.

Our situation is the same as yesterday.

It is now the seventh and we remain in this harbor. Today I thought about the white horses shown in the capital[7] at this season and found that the thought depressed me. The only white thing to be seen is the waves on the sea.

While I was thinking over such matters a long chest was delivered from a moor called "The Pond," which adjoins the house of a provincial official. Although it had such a name, there were not the usual pond-carp in the chest but parti-colored carp, rice, seafood, and other fine delicacies. Among them the most remarkable were young shoots, which reminded me that today is the day for gathering them. They came with a poem which read:

> Because miscanthus
> Grows rampant upon the moorfields,
>   These are young shoots
> That we have gathered from a "Pond"
> Where deep water is never to be found.

---

[6] It is unknown whether Masatsura or the other people mentioned by name in the *Diary* are real or fictional. The specification of names helps, however, to give an air of verisimilitude.

[7] The imperial showing of white horses and the gathering of young shoots were events associated with the New Year in the capital. Records suggest that the emperor did in fact order young shoots picked on the seventh day of the month of 734, as is suggested in the next paragraph. By the present calendar it would be mid-February, which accounts for the seemingly early appearance of flowers in the *Diary*.

The poem is clever enough. "The Pond" is a place-name for a locality to which a lady of distinguished family from the capital is said to have accompanied her husband to live.

Because the various contents of the chest were distributed to all the people of the ship, even to the young, people stuffed themselves with food, and the menials among the crew beat their bellies in contentment till the ocean must have been astonished and the waves led to rise.

So, a good deal has been happening all this while. To-day a strange person bearing a luncheon cabinet—his name slips my mind, but I shall recall it in a moment—this man came on purpose to recite a poem. After talking for some time, he read out a poem of address, speaking with some anxiety: "The waves really are running high!" His verses went:

> The white waves
> That will rise before you on the sea
>   Cry with loud voices,
> But I who am left behind you
> Shout louder far than they.

Such was his poem! He has recited it in a very loud voice— and just how can such verses compare with the good things he brought? Although people pretended to praise the strange presentation of the poem, no one composed a reply. There were many present who might have made a poem, but not one answered his. All anyone did was praise his verses and keep on eating till darkness fell, and so our poet said, "Don't expect me to wait forever!"

There was a young child of someone on the ship, who said rather bashfully, "Well, I'll give a poem in reply." We were all astonished but said, "Now that's very nice. Can you really make a poem? If you can, well, go right ahead." The child then asked, "Has he said he would leave? If he would have waited I would have recited a poem." Someone looked for our poet but, probably because it had grown so late, the man had already gone off after all. But being curious, the person asked the child, "What was the poem that you were going to speak?" Not unnaturally, the child was too shy to tell us, but after being pressed she spoke her verses.

> The river of tears
> Upon the sleeves of us who go
> And you who stay
> Just swells up upon its banks
> And makes them wetter all the time!

Surely the child acquitted herself well. It may be because she is so attractive, but she exceeded my expectations. Someone with her told her, "A child's poem is bound to have some faults. If you get some big person to help you, the results would really be nice. However it turns out, we shall send it to the man if we get a good chance to." Saying that, he appeared to copy down the poem.

The 8th.

Something untoward has prevented our departure, and so we remain in the same harbor. Tonight the moon is sinking into the sea. Seeing it do so, I find that verses by Lord Narihira[8] come to mind: "I wish the mountaintop would flee the moon / And delay the darkening of its light." If he had composed his poem by this seaside, might he not have written instead, "I wish the waves would rise so high / As to prevent the moon from sinking in the sea?" Alluding to Narihira's verses, someone composed a poem which went, I believe:

> As I look on the moon,
> Shining in its flowing across the sky,
> I see that the port-mouth
> Where the starry River of Heaven flows
> Is, like that of other streams, the sea.

Early in the morning on the ninth we left Ōminato, rowing on toward Naha harbor as our next stopping-place. Among the many, many people who came in succession to see us off and who said that they would accompany us

---

[8] Ariwara Narihira (825–880), one of the poets Tsurayuki singles out for notice in the Preface to the *Kokinshū*, appears again later in the *Diary*. See n. 24. The poem quoted from is *KKS*, I: 17.

just to the border of the province, there were Fujiwara Tokizane, Tachibana Suehira, Hasebe Yukimasa, and others. Since the day the former governor left his official residence, these men have devotedly followed us here and there, wherever we have gone. They are men warmly attached to the governor, with a depth of feeling not exceeded even by the depths of this sea.

From this harbor we shall at last be rowing on the open sea. It was for this final parting that those who followed us came to say farewell. Now as we row on, the people standing on the shore have grown remote, and the people aboard the ship have grown out of sight of those on land. They on the shore no doubt have things they wish to say to us, and we on the ship have words we would like to speak to them. It is no use. I did, however, murmur a poem to myself and find I had to leave it at that.

> It is my heart alone,
> Filled with distant thoughts of them,
> Which may cross the open sea,
> But since a letter cannot walk the waves,
> How can they know what I would say?

We now pass the pine grove on the coast of Uta. I cannot judge how many trees there must be or how many centuries they have stood there. During all this time, how the waves must have splashed on the roots of the trees, and the cranes have come and gone in its branches! It is impossible merely to look upon the splendor of this scenery,[9] and someone composed a poem something like this:

> Gazing all about,
> One can but believe the cranes
> Have been companions
> Of the pine trees upon whose tops
> They have nested through the ages.

To one looking upon the place itself, the poem falls far short of capturing the beauty of the scene.

---

[9] The idea that poetry comes from irrepressible feelings and that normal human beings wish to express their feelings in verse is a critical tenet of Tsurayuki in the Preface to the *Kokinshū* and is repeated effectively several times in the *Diary*, e.g., I. 20; II. 9 and 16.

I kept my attention on the beautiful sight ashore, and as the ship rowed on, the mountains, the sea, all darkened as night fell. One could not distinguish north from south and could only entrust the weather to the captain's understanding. Even a man unaccustomed to a sea voyage at night must find it disheartening. For a woman it was worse, nothing to do but hold one's head against the floor down in the boat and weep aloud. While I was so dejected, the men of the ship or the captain fell to singing boat songs till it could scarcely be borne. Two of the songs, one for a young wife and another for a peasant, went as follows:

> In the spring fields I cried aloud in pain—
> The young pampas grass had cut, had cut
>   my hands;
> I managed at last to pluck some shoots,
> And shall I take them to my parents?
> Will my mother-in-law make them a meal?
> And how can I get home!

> I wish I had caught the boy I met last night—
> I'll get his money, somehow;
> He told me a lie,
> He bought some things on promise,
> But he doesn't bring the money,
> He doesn't even come.

There were many songs besides these, but I shall not set them down. I heard people laughing over them, and although the sea was very rough, I felt somehow more at ease. We kept on in this way until we reached the harbor. An old man and an old woman in our group were not well and, unable to eat, had to keep to their pillows.

The 10th.
We spent the day in Naha harbor.

The 11th.
At dawn the boat set out for Murotsu. Since all of us were abed, we were unable to judge the appearance of the sea. But by the light of the moon we were able to make out our directions. As time passed, day broke into

full light; I washed up, and by the time I had done the
usual things of the morning, it was noon. Just then we
came upon Hane. Since it means "wings," a young child
asked, "Does this place called Hane look like bird's
wings?" It was just the sort of thing a child might ask, and
people were greatly amused. At this another child, a girl,
composed a poem.

> If it were only true,
> If the place would suit its name
> And provide us wings,
> Then we could climb upon the bird—
> Oh, to fly to the capital and home!

When the child inquired about this place called Hane,
my dead girl came at once to mind; in fact, when is it that
I forget her? Even more today, in my grief for my child
I think how our family is fewer in number than when we
set out from the capital. And when I recalled the old
poem[10] with its verses about the geese returning north—
"They have lost one from their number / As they wing
back to their home"—I composed some verses.

> Throughout this life,
> How much there is gives cause for grief,
> But the suffering
> That exceeds all other suffering
> Is to love and lose the child one loves.

When this was finished, I recited it over and over to myself. Truly . . .

The 12th.

It does not rain, though the sky is threatening. The ship
with Funtoki and Koremichi was delayed and separated
from ours, but they have come to Murotsu by way of
Narashizu.

Dawn on the thirteenth—a very light rain is falling.
After a short time it has stopped. A number of us women
said that we wished for the opportunity to bathe. We left

---

[10] A much-liked anonymous poem, *KKS*, IX: 412, an allegory by a
woman who had lost her husband in a province.

the ship and went ashore for a suitable place. While gazing upon the sea, I thought of a poem.

> White clouds and whitecaps,
> Both appear like foaming waves;
> Oh, for fisherfolk—
> Surely they can give me answer,
> Which are the white waves of the sea?

Because it is now after the tenth of the month, the moon
is bright. Since the day we first boarded the ship, I have
been unable to wear my lovely dark red robe. That must
not be done, I am told, out of danger of attracting the god
of the sea. Whatever the god of the sea may feel about
women and clothes,[11] and whether it is all right or not,
when I was bathing along the shore in a place scarcely
screened by reeds, I lifted the skirt of my robe to the point
of revealing my legs, and more that ought not to be seen.

The 14th.

Because rain has been falling since daybreak, we have
remained in the same harbor. This is a day of fast from
meat for the governor, but without the proper fast foods
on the boat, he is fasting for only half a day. Not having
ready money, he exchanged rice for sea-bream caught
yesterday by the captain of the ship, and after his fast
fell to eating the fish. There were others who had to do
such things on fast days. The captain has come again with
bream, and we exchange now rice, now sake for the food.
He is not displeased with the exchange.

The 15th.

We have no red beans to boil for January tonic. What a
pity.... Now with the weather bad again today, it is more
than twenty days since we began to creep along in this
boat. Because the days pass by so fruitlessly, we only look
about absentmindedly on the sea. A young girl composed
a poem.

---

[11] It was thought that women and highly colored clothes attracted the
sea-god and trouble. Similar superstitions exist in the West about women
aboard ship.

The wind may rise,
So do the waves, and so they fall
    With the falling wind;
They must be loving comrades,
The blowing wind and ceaseless waves.

Although it was the sort of undistinguished thing a child might write, it was apt enough for our situation.

The 16th.

Since the wind and waves have not subsided, we remain in the same place. I keep thinking that if only the sea would quiet, we could cross over to that place called Misaki. But the wind and waves are not likely to settle down very quickly. Looking at the surging waves—

It has been claimed
That this is so warm a province
    That frost never falls,
But still among the stormy waves
There falls the foaming snow.

So, today is the twenty-fifth day since we boarded the ship.

The 17th.

The dark clouds have at last cleared, and at a most lovely time just before dawn we set out rowing from the harbor. At this moment the region above the clouds and the depth of the sea appeared to shimmer together. It was probably a sight like this that led that man of ancient times to say, "The oar pierces the moon reflected on the waves, and the boat rests upon the sky shining on the sea."[12] But I am not certain that I heard or remember the quotation aright. Someone composed a poem along these lines.

Our ship is rowing
Upon the surface of the moon

_____

[12] The quotation she recites is a loose Japanese translation of two verses by Ku Tao (779–843), a minor T'ang poet. As a woman without Chinese, she has understood more than might have been expected. As the next poem shows, Japanese speak not of a man but of laurel in the moon.

> Lying in the waters,
> And that which catches back our oars
> Must be the laurel growing in the moon.

Hearing this, one of us composed another poem.

> The moon shines there,
> Deep among the waves that brighten
> With a celestial light,
> And as I row across the heavens
> I feel lost in all that great expanse.

As this was being said, it gradually became full day. And then suddenly the sailors cried out: "Black clouds have come up. There's sure to be a storm! The boat must turn back!" So we turned back, and on our way the rain began to fall. What a miserable time!

The 18th.

So, we are in the same harbor again. They are unable to take the boat out, because the sea has grown so rough. The harbor area itself is attractive as far as one can see. In this painful period of waiting to get home, however, it is impossible to appreciate the scene. Perhaps for a diversion, the men seem to have taken to reciting Chinese poems. Since we must somehow put up with the fact that the ship cannot set out, someone composed a poem.

> With a great banging
> The waves crowd in upon the shore,
> Which lies foaming white
> With a snow that always falls
> No matter what the month or year.

As the language shows, this poem was made by someone who does not usually compose verses. Someone else composed a poem.

> In the great waves
> Driven by the wind upon the shore,
> White flowers bloom
> Of a kind that neither the warbler
> Nor the spring could say it knew.

When he heard these two poems, the old man who is the leader of us passengers thought them to be rather interesting, and to beguile the great impatience we have all felt since last month, he too composed a poem.

> The ceaseless wind
> That drives the waves upon the shore
> And churns them white
> Seemed to have deceived the lookers-on,
> Who think the foam is snow or flowers.

While people were passing this or that judgment upon these poems, one person who had been listening most intently composed some verse himself. The poem was a misshapen thing, with too many syllables in the lines. At this no one was able to repress laughter. The person who composed it, however, was extremely irritated and full of complaint. Yet it was the kind of thing one could not pronounce aloud, and if one tried to set it down, it made no difference —one could still not parse it. If today it is hard to repeat the poem, what would it be like at some later time?

The 19th.
Because of bad weather, the boat is unable to set out.

The 20th.
With conditions like yesterday, the boat cannot leave. Everyone is worried over the situation and moping about. It is a terrible thing to have the days go by so slowly, and when I try to count the days that have passed, whether twenty or thirty, it is like breaking fingers in the count. Which only makes matters worse.

I am having great difficulty sleeping. The moon is in its twentieth night. There are no hills or mountains whose rim it might rise above, as it does in the capital, so it just seems to come out of the sea. It must have been just this kind of moon from the sea that, ages ago, was seen by Abe no Nakamaro from the coast of China. When he was returning to this country, at the place where he was to board the ship the men of that country gave him a farewell banquet and, in regret of his departure, composed proper Chinese poems

and performed other things for him. Perhaps because they
had not been able to express their reluctance to part ade-
quately, he stayed with them till the twentieth night of the
moon. His moon, too, must have risen from the sea. It was
on looking at it that Lord Nakamaro said, "In our country
we have composed poems since the age of the gods. The
gods themselves have done so, and now people of whatever
rank make poems of this kind to show their regret at parting and to express their joys or their sorrows." Telling them
of this, he composed the following poem.

> I cast my eyes
> Wide across the blue plains of the sea
> Brilliant with a moon—
> Can it be the one that in far Kasuga
> Rises over the hilltop of Mikasa?[13]

So it went. The men of that country were unable to appreciate it, but when the chief features of its meaning were
written in Chinese and sketched in outline, and when they
had had it interpreted for them, they were able to judge its
feeling and appreciated it to an extent unforeseen. China
and this country have different languages, but since the radiance of the moon is the same for both, men's feelings
about it must surely be the same. The recollections of that
distant age led to a poem.

> This is the very moon
> That we see upon the mountain's rim
> In the capital,
> But here the moon arises from the waves
> And back into the waves it sets.

The 21st.

About six o'clock in the morning the boat set out at last.
The boats of our fellow travelers also left. As I looked

---

[13] The poem of Abe no Nakamaro (698–770) given here is adapted
from the version in *KKS*, IX: 406, where the first line reads *Ama no hara*,
"the wide plains of the sky," rather than "the blue plains of the sea." Mr.
Kubota Hiroshi, a high-school teacher at Muroto, told Professor Konishi
that a pupil had pointed out that at this season the moon cannot in fact
be seen to rise from the sea, as the poem implies. Both changes reveal
Tsurayuki shaping materials into art.

at the scene of the boats on the water, it was as though
the leaves of autumnal trees had scattered in the early
spring sea. Was it because of the strength of our unceas-
ing prayers? At all events, the wind did not blow, and we
rowed out in fine weather. At this time a child whom we
had asked to serve our group sang a boat song.

> Always I look back
> Toward my native place,
> To where my parents are,
> And how can I get home?

His song touched the feelings of us all. As he was singing
and the boat bore on, we passed a place where dark-colored
birds were gathered upon the tops of rocks along the coast,
while the waves shattered white at their base. It was as the
captain said: "The white waves are heading where the
black birds roost." There was nothing very special about
his words, but at the time they sounded like the verse of a
poem. Since it was not the sort of thing one would expect a
sea captain to say, it caught one's attention.

As we were bearing on during these remarks, our leader
was looking out upon the waves. All the way from Tosa he
had been saying that we were in danger of encountering
pirates. The sea is a terrifying element to one with such ap-
prehensions, and his hair has all gone white as a result. It
is the sea that has made him age to seventy or eighty.

> On his head a snow,
> On the rocky coast white waves
> Falling constantly—
> Tell me, which of those is whiter,
> You guardian of these isles.

Captain, you should repeat this poem to the guardian of
the isles!

The 22nd.

We are heading from the harbor where we stopped last
night to another. The mountains can be seen in the distance. There was a boy of about eight—he looks younger
than his real age—who saw that as the ship rowed onward

the mountains also seemed to move. He thought it very strange and made some verses.

> As I look out
> From the ship that rows along,
>   With their sloping sides
> The mountains themselves move along;
> But do the pines upon them know?

Such was his poem, and as the composition of a child it was very appropriate.

Today, with the roughness of the sea, it is as though snow is falling on the beach and wave-flowers are blossoming. Someone made a poem.

> All the ear can hear
> Is the single sound of waves,
>   But to see their color
> —Of snow, or is it blossoms?
> Brings confusion to one's eyes.

The 23rd.

The sun was shining, but afterwards the sky clouded over. Since there is danger of pirates in this vicinity, we prayed to the gods and the Buddha.

The 24th.

We are in the same place as yesterday.

The 25th.

Since the captain and sailors say that a north wind is unfavorable,[14] they will not set forth. All that one hears is that pirates will come after us.

The 26th.

Whether or not it is true, it is said that pirates were looking for us, and therefore about midnight the boat slipped out in the dark. As we rowed on our way, we came to the place of supplication for safety.[15] On the captain's order,

---

[14] A north wind would be adverse to travelers heading northward along the east side of Shikoku toward the Kinki area of Honshu.

[15] It is not known what kind of place this was, or where, but since land travelers normally prayed at the top of slopes, it was probably at some prominent coastal place familiar to sailors.

FIG. 6. Map of the Journey of *The Tosa Diary*
Simplified to show major verifiable places.

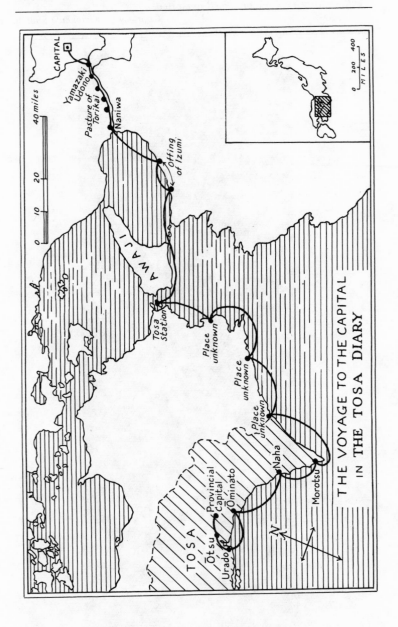

FIG. 7. An Ocean-going Ship
From Kitano Tenjin Engi *(Thirteenth Century).*
Tenth-century ships are presumed to be similar.

Courtesy of Kadokawa Shoten

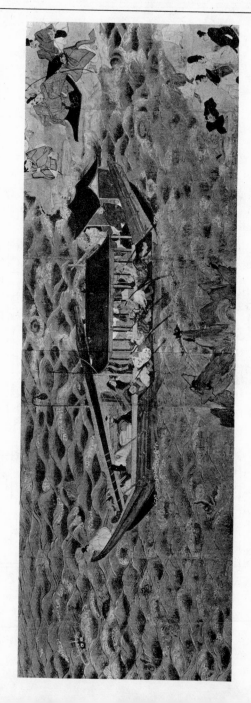

the sacred offering of shredded cloth[16] was raised up. As it fell to the east, the captain spoke the words of offering: "May the boat speed on in the direction this offering has fallen." With these words he performed the rite. Hearing what he had said, a girl made some verses.

> O wind that blew
> The offering at the place of supplication
> To the god that guards
> Our passage on the ocean paths,
> Blow steadily till we reach our home.

Since the condition of the wind was favorable at this time, the captain, with great swaggering, had the sail raised. He was mightily pleased. When we heard the sound inside our quarters, the children and the older women, whose thoughts were only about getting home, rejoiced greatly. Among the group was one called the Old Woman of Awaji, who composed a poem.

> Now that the wind has risen,
> The sound of hands clattering up a sail
> To speed on our ship
> Is one that brings a flutter to our hearts
> And makes us strike our hands for joy.

We prayed that we might continue in fair weather.

The 27th.

With the wind too high, the seas have grown rough and our boat cannot set out. Everyone is extremely dejected. Hearing that as an amusement the men were reciting Chinese verses, including, "As I gaze upon the sun, the capital seems to grow more and more remote," a woman who had understood the gist of the line made a poem.

> Although the sun
> That should be so far away is seen
> Hard by the clouds,
> The capital to which I would return
> Lies remote upon our distant road.

---

[16] The sacred offering (*nusa*) might also be shredded paper or bark and was a Shinto offering associated with journeys.

The wind blew hard all day. I snapped my fingers in irritation and fell asleep.

The 28th.

Throughout the night rain fell unceasingly. This morning, too.

The 29th.

The boat has set out again. The sun is shining gloriously and the boat rows along smartly. Observing that my nails have grown extremely long, and counting the days, I discovered that today is the Day of the Rat; thinking that to clip them would be unpropitious, I did not do so. Since it is January, I mentioned the Festival of the Day of the Rat[17] in the capital. "If only we had just a little pine tree for the occasion," I said. But since we are on the sea, what good would that do? A certain woman showed us a poem she had written.

> It avails us little
> But today is the Festival of the Rat—
> If a fisherwoman,
> I would have at least a celebration
> In cutting the poor pine weeds of the sea.[18]

What can one say in favor of a poem on the Festival of the Rat—at sea? Another person recited a poem.

> This is just the time,
> But I shall not go out to pick
> The young shoots of the day,
> Because the waters that we row across
> Are far from being the fields of Kasuga.

We kept rowing on while the poem was being recited. The ship was steered by a place of exceptional beauty. When I

---

[17] The Festival was associated with the appreciation of pine trees, which were thought long-lived and propitious. Like hours of the day, days of the month and years ran on cycles of such zodiacal signs as the Rat, the Horse, etc. The Day of the Ox was thought best for clipping fingernails, the Day of the Tiger for toenails. In theory at least, such notions governed the lives of Japanese in the Heian period.

[18] *Umimatsu*, or sea pine, is a variety of seaweed, the fanciful if inadequate marine equivalent of the pines used in the festival at the capital.

asked, "What place is this?" the answer was, "The Tosa Station." A woman on the ship who had lived in former days in yet another place called Tosa said, "In the past I lived for a time in a place with the same name! What an odd feeling." And I composed a poem.

> For how long was it
> That I lived once in a distant place
> That bore this very name?
> It moves the heart to think that now
> The waves of Tosa wash upon the ship.

The 30th.

There is no rain, and the wind is still. Hearing that pirates do not venture out at night, we set forth about midnight and crossed to the Whirlpool of Awa. Since it was the middle of the night, we could not distinguish north from south. Men and women alike we prayed desperately to the gods and the Buddha and at last passed through the whirlpool. We went by Nushima in the early dawn and then crossed past Tanagawa. Making as much haste as possible, we arrived at the Offing of Izumi. Today the ocean is so still as to have nothing resembling waves. It seems that we have received the favor of the gods and the Buddha.

Today, on counting the number of days since we boarded ship, I see that it has been thirty-nine. Since we have now come to Izumi province, there is no longer danger from pirates.

SECOND MONTH. The 1st.

It rained throughout the morning. The sky having cleared about noon, we rowed out along the Offing of Nada. Like yesterday, there is neither wind nor rain at sea. We are passing the pine groves of Kurosaki: since the name means "Black Point," that is one color. The color of the pines is green. The waves upon the coast are like snow, and the seashells are scarlet. Only yellow is lacking from the Five Shades. Today we have begun to pull a dragnet from a place called Hako Bay. While we are proceeding in this fashion, someone made a poem about this "Box Bay."

> Fit for a jeweled comb,
> The box of Hako where the bay-waves
> Do not rise upon the sea—
> Surely all would think on such a day
> The sea a mirror fit for such a box.

The response of our leader to the scene was to sigh, "To think that it is the Second Month already . . ." There seemed to be no interruption to the misery of travel, and so from what seemed deep feeling he added the following poem:

> The boat goes on,
> The spring day stretches out as long
> As the dragnet pulled behind,
> And somehow I have managed to pull out
> Some forty or fifty dragging days at sea.

Someone who had heard the leader whispered: "Now listen to that—it's no better than prose. He comes out with some fumbling words and thinks himself a very clever poet. Of course he might be offended if he heard what we think." The whispering continued for a time and then broke off.

Because the wind suddenly rose and the waves grew rough, we stopped for mooring.

The 2nd.

The wind and rain are increasing. Through the day and through the night we prayed to the gods and the Buddha.

The 3rd.

With the condition of the sea the same as yesterday, the boat cannot set out. With no letup to the wind, the surf breaks in on the shore and then flows back. I have set down a poem about this.

> Twisting up hemp,
> I spin a thread that has no use;
> It is because the tears
> Whose beads fall heavily each day
> Are not such jewels as might be strung.

With matters in this state, night has come.

The 4th.

The captain said, "The condition of the wind and the sky is extremely unfavorable," so that it has not been possible to put out the boat. All the same, neither the wind nor the waves rose so high. This captain really seems unable to tell anything about the weather. On the shore of this harbor there are many beautiful little shells and pebbles. For all their beauty, because they are just the sort of thing she would have liked to gather, they remind me of my little girl who has passed away. I made a poem.

> Beating upon the shore,
> O waves, I wish that you would bring
> Shells of forgetfulness
> That I might pick a shell of comfort
> From the heavy thoughts of her I love.

When I spoke the poem, there was one with us who was unable to remain silent and made a poem on the sufferings of our voyage.

> Shells of forgetfulness—
> Not they the things I shall take up,
> But pretty pebbles
> To remind me of a precious child,
> To be a souvenir of her I loved.

No doubt a parent becomes almost a distraught child in grieving for her daughter, and someone may well say, "The girl could not have been such an incomparable treasure." For all that, the proverb is true: "A lost child is always lovely." So it goes. The day has passed at the same place, and a woman with us composed a poem:

> If Izumi province
> Were a spring and not a name alone,
> My dipping hand
> Would feel the cold and not be empty
> As the days that pass by on these shores.

The 5th.

Today at long last we leave the Offing of Izumi for the harbor at Ozu. The pine grove stretches off and off along the land. Everyone thought the endless sight depressing, and I therefore composed a poem.

> Although we move,
> Still we seem as endless in our motion
> As a spinning wife,
> Spinning the thread of the Ozu shore
> Where the endless pine groves stretch.

As I repeated this to myself, our leader pressed the captain: "Let's hurry and row out in this fine weather!" The captain told his men: "We have our orders. Let us make haste with the ship. Pull hard on the towrope, before the morning calm is over, and the wind blows from the north." These words, which fell into the cadence of a poem were the very words the captain spoke. Of course he had no idea that he had spoken anything like a poem. On hearing him, I said, "This sounds strangely like a poem." Copying down the words, I found that they really fit into the meter of a poem.

Throughout the day we prayed, "Let the waves be still today," and the sea was calm. Just now we passed an area where gulls had gathered and were cavorting. Because this was a sign that we were approaching the main island and nearing the capital, a child composed a poem in a burst of joy.

> Thanks to our prayers,
> It seemed there was a letup in the wind—
> But all in vain,
> Because the very gulls themselves
> Alight like waves so white upon the beach.

As this was being said, we rowed on until we came to a place called Ishizu, which had lovely pine groves. The shoreline lay stretched out in the distance, and we continued along it to the coast of Sumiyoshi.[19] Someone made a poem.

---

[19] Sumiyoshi and Suminoe ("Sumi Inlet") are often used interchangeably as place-names. The "grasses of forgetfulness" (*wasuregusa*) mentioned later were traditionally associated with Sumiyoshi (cf. Mibu no Tadamine's poem, *KKS*, XVIII: 917).

> Now that I see them,
> I have come to understand myself.
> Ages-old the pines
> And green upon the Sumi Inlet,
> But I before them white with years.

Hearing this, one like myself the mother of a dead girl, naturally found it impossible to forget her, even for part of a day. My poem:

> O take our ship
> To rest upon the beach of Sumiyoshi!
> For I would like to pick
> The grasses of forgetfulness to see
> If they can prove the promise of their name.

My intention was not that I should utterly forget, but that just for a moment I might rest my aching heart and then return with renewed strength for loving her.

As I was whispering this poem, lost in my thoughts while gazing out from the ship, the wind suddenly blew up. Although the crew rowed and rowed, the stern of the ship only dipped and bobbed till with the danger it seemed that we would be swallowed by the sea. The captain said, "The great god of Sumiyoshi is like other gods. Surely there is something he desires"—all this being pronounced in a mincing, would-be fashionable voice. "Someone present him with sacred shredded cloth," he ordered. The offering was given as he said. In spite of the presentation, the wind did not abate at all; on the contrary, the gale rose and the waves grew yet rougher. At this the captain declared, "If the god's heart is unstirred, the ship will not stir, either. It seems we have got to present him with something that suits him." He continued, "There's nothing else to be done. As they say, we have two good eyes, but—we will offer him one mirror." As he said this, he threw a valuable mirror into the sea.[20] It was a great loss. But even as it was done,

---

[20] Mirrors were made of metal with embossed obverse sides. For centuries they had been regarded as treasures and were among the earliest Japanese imports from the mainland. As the earlier poem on Hako Bay shows, they were kept in special boxes. The preceding sentence recalls the proverb, "We have two eyes but one thing more precious," sometimes meaning a child. Here it refers to the mirror.

the sea became as smooth as the surface of a mirror, leading someone to compose a poem.

> Mighty he is,
> The god whose heart was raging
>   With the wild sea,
> Yet when we gave the mirror to the waves,
> They and his heart reflected calm.

What an experience it was . . .

The things associated with this place—the calm sea of Sumiyoshi, the grasses of forgetfulness of care, and the elegant princess-pines of the shore—the god resembles none of them. It was plain to see that the god's desire was reflected in that mirror and that the mind of the captain understood that of the god.

The 6th.

We went past the boundary-marker of the harbor[21] and, arriving after so long at Naniwa,[22] we started into the mouth of the Yodo River. Without exception everyone, including the old men and women, clapped their hands about their heads for joy. Hearing that we had at last come in from the sea, the Old Woman of Awaji, who had suffered so much from seasickness throughout the voyage, in her joy raised her head from where she had been lying on the floor of the ship and made a poem.

> With downcast heart,
> I asked, how long, how long this trip,
>   And now at Naniwa
> Our ship has come at last from open sea,
> Cutting its way through reeds of the lagoon.

Since she was the last person one would expect to compose such a poem, the people on the boat greeted her poem with surprise. Among them hearing the poem was our lead-

---

[21] The boundary-marker (*miotsukushi*) is a device to indicate for navigational purposes the level of water and as such is translated "the flood gauge" by Arthur Waley, *The Tale of Genji*, II, v. But the point here is that in entering past the marker, the travelers have come from open sea into the port.

[22] Naniwa is the old name for what has become Osaka. As the next poem shows, reeds were associated with the area.

er who, although troubled by his illness, said with great consideration, "Since your face is so drawn by seasickness, we had not thought you could make so good a poem."

The 7th.

As we entered the mouth of the river today and started upstream, the water became very shallow. What a situation! It was next to impossible for the boat to make headway. While this was happening, our leader, who is a sick man, decided that since the Old Woman of Awaji had composed a poem and since we were nearing the capital, he might compose one, too. He did so in spite of the fact that he has never known much of anything about so refined an occupation as poetry, and with considerable effort he brought out a most peculiar poem.[23]

> Here we are, we are,
> But because the riverway upstream
> Is grown too shallow,
> Neither the boat nor I myself
> Can call this a day free from pain.

That is the sort of poem a person would compose because he is ill. Since one poem was not enough to satisfy his feelings, there was another.

> That keeping
> Our ship from speeding as I like
> Is that in its bed
> The water of the stream is shallow,
> And shallow-hearted, too, to me.

It appears that he made this poem because he was unable to contain his joy at nearing the capital. But the poems were clumsier than that of the Old Woman of Awaji. He regretted his poetic efforts. "It's exasperating!" he said. "It would have been better if I had not made the poems." Meanwhile night had come on, and I soon fell asleep.

The 8th.

It is only with great difficulty that we have been able to

---

[23] The leader or *funagimi* ("lord of the boat") is identified by most Japanese scholars with the former governor, the *persona* of Tsurayuki. That is possible but, as this episode shows, the leader is a very halting poet, unlike the former governor on XII. 26.

move upstream and to come for a stop at a place called the
Meadow of Torikai. This evening our leader had an out-
break of his chronic illness and suffered greatly. Someone
brought fresh fish, and we gave rice in return. The men
seem to be whispering among themselves about it. "To
get fresh fish for rice is to catch a whale with a shrimp,"
said one of them. But such things happen everywhere.
Since today is a fast day for us, it is: no fish.

The 9th.

Because we were so impatient, we set forth before dawn,
but no matter how hard the boat was towed, what with
the lack of water in the river, we barely scraped along.
Creeping onward, we came to a place called the Fork of
Wada, where we ordered rice, fish, and other things for
breaking fast.

These things done, our boat was towed farther upstream, and as we went along we were looking upon a
place called the Palace of Nagisa. When one thinks of
former times, this palace has a special charm. On a hill to
the rear of it there is a stand of pines, and plum trees were
in blossom in the central garden. While we were there,
someone said, "This was a famous place in former days.
It is the place where the Commander of the Horse
Guards,[24] Ariwara Narihira, enjoyed the company of
Prince Koretaka and composed his poem:

> If in this world
> There ever was a time when cherry trees
>   Failed in the blossoming,
> Then the responsive hearts of men
>   Might answer to a tranquil spring.[25]

---

[24] The title actually given Narihira is *chūjō*, whose modern equivalent
is lieutenant general. In the *Ise Monogatari*, the hero (modeled on
Narihira) is called at one point "Commander of the Horse Guards of
the Right," and the phrase has seemed to suggest the social position of
Narihira more accurately than "lieutenant general." Both for reasons of
family loyalty and of personal attachment, Narihira was on close terms
with Prince Koretaka, who was kept from the throne by powerful intrigue,
in spite of his father's desire to have him designated heir.

[25] Narihira's poem may be found, with a variation in the third line, in
KKS, I: 53. Abe no Nakamaro from the eighth century and Narihira
from the ninth are the only two historical, named poets in the *Diary*. Their
poems are famous for expressing depth of feeling about natural phenomena, and so fit the chief poetic principle of the *Diary*.

One person with us today composed a poem appropriate to the location.

> Here are the pine trees
> That have passed through countless ages;
> Still the breezes blow
> Rustling through them with a voice
> Unchanged in coolness from the past.

Another person made a poem.

> Loved by the Prince,
> And standing at a palace ages old,
> The flowering plum
> Still sends forth its faithful odor,
> The very fragrance of the past.

As this was being recited, we continued upstream in great happiness at nearing the capital.

Among those on the boat were a number of people who had had children born to them during service in Tosa, although none but me had taken a child along. At one place where the boat was moored today, these parents took their children in their arms, lifting them on and off the boat. Seeing this, I thought with unrelieved heartache of my dead girl.

> Those who had none
> When we went down to the province
> Now return with children,
> While I who had one had her die
> And now come home with only grief.

Saying this, I fell to weeping. And what would be her father's thoughts if he heard my verses? I do not set down these words, nor did I compose the poem, out of mere love of writing.[26] Surely both in China and in Japan art is that which is created when we are unable to suppress our feelings.

---

[26] The sentence is perhaps the most obscure of several uncertain ones in the *Diary*. In this instance I have left the commentators and made a distinction between the prose words (*koto*) of the *Diary* and the poem (*uta*) just quoted. It is possible, however, that the distinction made by Professor Konishi in his edition (p. 183) between the poem just given and poetry in general is the best one. There are other glosses as well.

Tonight we stopped at a place called Udono.

The 10th.

Today being ominous, we did not continue the journey.

The 11th.

After raining a little, it has stopped. As we started up-stream I noticed that toward the east there lay a line of low-stretched hills. When I inquired about this of some-one, I was told that it was the Shrine of Yawata. When we heard we had come so close to the capital, we were over-joyed and gave prayers of thanks. The Bridge of Yama-zaki[27] came into view and at this our joy was unbounded. Here, near Sōō Temple, our boat was stopped and there were various consultations. The willows grow in profusion on the banks near this temple. Seeing the reflection of the willows deep in the stream, someone made a poem.

> The rippling waves
> Flow softly in their rich design.
> Are they not woven
> From the threads in this reflection
> Of fine green willows on the shore?

The 12th.

We are stopping in Yamazaki.

The 13th.

Still at Yamazaki.

The 14th.

It is raining. Men have been sent to the capital for carts.

The 15th.

The carts have come. Glad to be free of the constrictions of the boat, we have left it for a certain person's house. At this house we had, what pleased us greatly, excellent and proper food. With so generous a host and such fine hos-pitality, the past weeks seem even more distasteful. We

---

[27] Yamazaki Bridge marked the end of travel by boat up the Yodo River and so was a welcome sight.

exchanged numerous gifts. The manners of our hosts are faultless.

The 16th.

At dusk today we started for the capital, and as we went I observed that neither the shop-sign of little boxes in Yamazaki nor that of the great hook in Magari had changed.[28] But people seemed to wonder whether the disposition of the merchants had altered for the better.

As we were proceeding toward the capital, one person came to Shimasaka[29] to bid us welcome. This was an act that was not required of him. Indeed there were many more people who did this or that for us when we came back than those who did things for us as we left. We presented gifts in return to these people.

We had decided to enter the capital after dark,[30] and were in no great hurry. As we went slowly along the moon rose and we crossed the Katsura River to the capital in moonlight. People were talking about the river. "Since it is not like the changeable Asuka River,[31] its depths and shallows are just where they were before." And another person recited a poem.

> From the wide heavens,
> The laurel-figured moon shines down,
>   On the Katsura River,
> And even its radiance is unchanged,
> Brightening the very bottom of the stream.

---

[28] Another obscure passage. The translation here follows the interpretation involving antithesis in the ideas of little, great; boxes, hook; etc. See Suzuki, ed., p. 76.

[29] Shimasaka is the place where returning travelers would cross the Katsura River into the limits of the capital.

[30] It was common to end journeys at night, and also—as the first entry in the *Diary* shows—so to begin them.

[31] The Asuka River in Yamato province is famous in poetry for its changeable course, as the punning poem alluded to (*KKS*, XVIII: 933) shows.

> This world's course—
> What is in it that is constant?
>   Tomorrow River
> Yesterday streamed in depths where
> Today its shallows flow.

(Translation taken from Robert H. Brower and Earl Miner, *Japanese Court Poetry*, Stanford, London, 1961.)

Another person recited a poem.

> The Katsura River—
> All this time as distant in my mind
> As high-floating clouds,
> But though your waves have wet my sleeves,
> Have I not crossed at last to home?

Yet another person composed a poem.

> The Katsura River
> Cannot be said to flow upon a course
> Taken through my heart,
> But it is flowing in depths the same
> As the depths of happiness I feel.

Just as our joy for the capital grew excessive, so too the number of poems was over-many to set down. It had now become dark, and we were unable to see the various places we longed to. Yet how good it is to be back in the capital!

Arriving at our house and entering the gate, we could see everything clearly in the bright moonlight. All the same, even though we had heard something of it, we found the house fallen in and dilapidated beyond words. The heart of the person to whom we had entrusted the house must have gone to ruin, too. There is after all the familiar inner hedge—it *must* be the same house that we entrusted with such hope while we were away. It was because of such hopes that we had sent back gifts at every opportunity. In spite of all, I restrained our people from saying, "What a mess this is—hadn't we sent gifts all the time?" Although the attitude of our manager was most distasteful, we shall pay him thanks.

There is one place where water has collected like a pond. There are even new pines growing at its edge. In the five or six years that we were away, centuries seem to have transpired here. Half the property has disappeared, and everything is jumbled with new growth. Since for the most part things are in ruin, people are saying, "What a pity it all is."

Innumerable feelings press upon me and among them the dearest are thoughts of the girl who was born in this house. It is impossible to say how broken-hearted I am that she has not returned with us. Those who were with us on the boat now have children swarming about and making commotion. My unhappiness seemed to find no relief amid all this bustle, so I composed a poem I did not tell to the others.

> She was born here,
> And although she did not return,
>   When back in this house
> I look upon the little pines grown here
> With grief for one who grows no more.

Since I still had not exhausted my feelings, I wrote down another poem.

> The girl I daily saw—
> If she might have lived like pine trees
>   Through the centuries,
> Why should she have left in that far place
> On the distant parting of eternity?

I could not forget her if I wished to, and there are so many other reasons for being unhappy that I cannot exhaust them by setting them down. It really is best that I should tear up these papers and end at once.

The Diary
of Izumi Shikibu
(*Izumi Shikibu Nikki*)
attributed to Izumi Shikibu

The Diary
of Izumi Shikibu

Day seemed to follow day unnoticed as she grieved for the loss of a world of love that had proved more fleeting than a dream, and it was already past the 10th of the Fourth Month[1] as shadows gathered under the trees so freshly leaved. On the earthen wall across the garden the grasses were a luxuriant green, not a sight to arrest the attention of anyone else but enough to cause her to fall into a fast reverie. Then it appeared that someone was approaching through a nearby gap in the fence. As she was wondering who it might be, it turned out to be the Page in the service of the late prince. Since he had come just when she was so deeply stirred, she had a message conveyed to him by one of her women: "Why has it been so long since you have come here? Especially since I have wished so much for a reminder of what now seems so long ago."

He replied at some length. "I hesitated to do so because I thought you might take offense at my familiarity if I called on you without any special purpose. In addition I have recently been on a pilgrimage to a mountain temple and simply have not been able to come. I have been left, idle and drifting, with no one to rely upon for support, so that thinking it might be some substitute for seeing the late prince, I have now entered the service of his younger brother, the Prince Governor-General."

"Now that is good news," she said. "But isn't your new

---

1 The beginning of the *Diary* is dated A.D. 1003 by the commentators, assuming the references here to be to real events, the chief of which is the "loss" occasioned by the death of Prince Tametaka, who had been Izumi Shikibu's lover till he died in 1002. The 10th of the Fourth Month is late May by our reckoning.

prince rather dignified and stiff. Surely things are not the way they were with Prince Tametaka?"

"That is true," he said, "but still the Prince is a warm-hearted person. He asked me in fact, 'You visit the Lady, don't you?' When I said I have come here on occasion, he said, 'Take some of these flowers with you. Give them to her and see what she thinks of them.' " So he presented the orange flowers. Without thinking, she murmured the lines, "I am reminded of the scented sleeves / And wonder about that person of my past."[2]

"I must be going," the Page said. "Is there any message you wish me to take to His Highness?" It was awkward to put a message into words. But she had never heard any criticism of the reliability of the Prince and so, although it represented no great commitment on her part, she sent a poem.

> Rather than recall
> The fragrance of the by-gone orange blossoms,
>   Oh, you wood thrush,
> I should like to hear your singing
> To determine if your voice is also true.

It appears that the Prince had remained at the edge of his verandah, and when he saw the Page lingering under cover with a significant look on his face, he asked, "What happened, then?" To this, the Page handed over the poem. The Prince wrote a poem in reply.

> When the wood thrush
> Can acquaint you with its singing
>   On the accustomed bough,
> You will discover that its voice
> Speaks with unvaried truth.

When he had written this, he told the Page, "Say nothing of this to anyone. It would only seem licentious." With this he entered the building. When the Page had delivered the message to her, she found it gave her pleasure. Could she

---

[2] A very apposite recollection of an anonymous poem, *KKS*, III: 139, recalling the lover she has lost.

expect that they would continue to write back and forth?
She wondered but sent no reply.

Once he began to send letters, they came in succession.
There was a poem.

> The words unspoken,
> All that was in my heart was confided
> Only in small part;
> Such suppression brings a greater pain
> To the anguish of this grieving day.

Being somewhat imprudent by nature and unaccustomed
to the hours of tedium she had lived through recently, she
found her heart engaged even by so uncommitted a thing
as his poem, and therefore she replied:

> Imagine if you will,
> You with that heart of yours in anguish
> On one grieving day,
> What it is like to be another heart
> Spending a whole life in tedious reverie.

In such fashion he sent letters with some frequency, and
from time to time she replied to them. Time passed, and
she found in the correspondence some diversion from her
meaningless days. Then another letter came, written in
more detail than the previous ones.

> Might you not find
> Some cause for consolation to your heart
> If we could talk at ease?
> Yet do not think me to be a person
> Whose worth consists in only words.

He added, "How would this evening be as a chance for
the two of us to chat about all those things that really
interest us?" To this she replied:

> I do indeed desire
> Some consolation for my heart,
> As you ask to speak,

But I am one whose life has suffered
And its worth consists not even of words.

"My sobbing is endless, like the rustle of reeds. Even if I saw you, what good could it do?"[3]

Thinking quite rightly that she could have little idea of his intentions, from about noon he began to prepare for a visit to her. At last, he called to him a trusted lieutenant of the Right Guards: "Let us be off, in disguise." The officer thought, "Ah yes, he'll be going to that lady's house."

He came in a carriage that would have been sumptuous for an ordinary person, and had his arrival announced. When she heard of this she felt very ill at ease, but she could scarcely say, "I am not at home." She had after all replied to his poem during the day, and it seemed heartless to turn him away when she was actually at home. But she would allow nothing except conversation. She therefore had him admitted at the western entry and had a round cushion set out for him. Although she was perhaps influenced by what people said of him, as she regarded him from behind her curtains she thought him out of the ordinary and in fact unusually distinguished. Their conversation was rather constrained, but as they spoke of various things, the moon rose and made the night very bright.

He said, "I am an old-fashioned and retiring sort not used to such a bright place. Since I find myself very ill at ease in this spot, please let me come inside to where you are sitting. You can be sure, in spite of what you may be thinking, that I have no intention of behaving hereafter as men usually do."

"What is this?" she replied at once. "Tonight is the only time I expect to be talking with you like this. I don't know what you mean by your 'hereafter.'"

The night grew very late as they talked so fruitlessly. "At this rate it will soon be dawn," he said, adding a poem.

---

[3] The poem and the prose remark allude both to the Prince's poem and to a poem by Yamabe Akahito (d. ?736) in *Kokin Rokujō*, III (*Zoku Kokka Taikan*, 32, 545). The multiple allusions suggest considerable sensitivity—and self-possession—even while the words express hopeless grief.

> I have not possessed
> Anything even so fleeting as a dream,
> And now dawn breaks—
> What is there left for me to recall
> In conversation on a later night?

To that she replied:

> As the night comes
> My sleeves grow wet in recollection,
> And first and last
> I know this world holds no future chance
> For me to have a peaceful dream of love.

"Really, much less tonight . . . ," she murmured.

"You must not think I am one who wastes my time in ceaseless ramblings at night," he countered, "even if you do not think very tenderly of me. But I like you so much I am almost frightened by it." And he quietly entered behind her curtains. She was wholly at a loss what to think, but he pledged himself with so many promises and, just as light broke in the sky, he returned to his palace.

His next-morning letter soon came.[4] "I have just returned and wonder how you are. It is very strange—I can turn my mind to nothing but you." And his poem,

> Perhaps you think
> That as I spoke of love I intended
> Only what others mean,
> But my heart is filled this morning
> With an unrivalled truth of love.

She sent an answer.

> I do not think
> That this love can only signify
> What others mean by love:
> This morning I have learnt at last
> What it truly means to be in love.

---

[4] This episode reveals something of the practice of courtly love. When the lady did not ignore or altogether refuse him, the lord could try his luck. He would go at dusk in disguise and, with words, action, and good fortune, might win the lady. He would leave about dawn and was required to send a next-morning letter. Much depended thereafter on the lady's success in holding his affections.

For all that, how dubious her actions were! And to think how the late prince had loved her. While her thoughts were in such confusion, the familiar Page called on her. Surely he had brought her a letter. Discovering that he did not, she found her misery complete. It was the last disgrace.[5] The Page was going back, so she sent a message by him.

> Even waiting for you,
> Would my heart be agitated so?
> I do not expect you,
> And yet my heart anguishes in yearning
> As today the twilight hour comes.

When he read the poem he thought that it was a pity she suffered so, but his actions were handicapped by his lack of prior experience of going out at night.

His Consort was not a person given to a woman's usual intimacy with her husband, but she did regard nocturnal goings and comings with suspicion. She could not regard in a friendly light the activities of the late prince, who encountered criticism till the end of his life for his attachment to this Lady, and even if he conducted himself circumspectly, would it not be a sign that he did not really love his Consort?

Just as darkness fell his reply came.

> If you tell me
> That you wait with all your heart,
> You will not then find
> That I am slow in setting forth
> On the path that takes me to your house.

"Do not think," he urged, "that I am trifling with you." "Not at all," she answered, "and as for me,"

> Though you do not come,
> I am far from any doubt or care
> Over such a fact,
> For, from other worlds, you and I
> Have been fast bound by fate to love.

---

[5] She feels shame for infidelity to the memory of Prince Tametaka and, in addition, infers from the lack of a letter that Prince Atsumichi has betrayed her, probably thinking her behavior wanton.

"That is what I try to think, but without some comfort from you, I feel I shall melt away like dew."[6] He intended to come, but unaccustomed as he was to deal with such a matter, he let days pass without a visit.

On the last day of the month she sent him a poem.

> Oh, my wood thrush,
> Your endearing voice is hidden
> From our busy world,
> And if again today I miss you,
> When can I hope to hear your song?[7]

He was in such numerous company that he was unable to read the message for some time. When it was brought to him the next morning, he replied:

> If its low voice
> Is one that brought you anguish,
> Listen now again,
> For from today the wood thrush
> Sings in a louder voice and true.

Two or three days later he visited her in disguise. But she had resolved to make a pilgrimage. While she was busy with the necessary purifications, she thought how his neglect revealed his lack of real interest in her. Even though he was here, she scarcely spoke to him, using her devotions as a pretext. A letter came from him the next morning. "This is the morning after a peculiar lovers' night," he protested, with more in that vein.

> Since I was born
> I have never known of such a way
> For two fast lovers,
> For though we met, we did not really meet
> And dawn broke on our separation.

---

[6] These words expand upon two in the original that allude to an anonymous poem, GSS, XIV: 1,032.

[7] It is past the end of the Fourth Month, when the wood thrush (*hototogisu*) still sings with a lovely low voice. The bird of course represents the Prince, recalling his first poem. We may infer from the image of the wood thrush that rather more than a month has passed since the Page came bearing orange flowers.

"I could not have believed it," he added.

It really did seem too bad, and, in a similar mood of regret, she replied.

> As each night comes,
> I fall into a yearning for your visit,
> But the night still fails
> To bring that loving meeting of the eyes
> To one whose vows have made her wife.

"Unfortunately, there is nothing at all unusual about a day we do not meet," she added.

He wrote the next day. "Are you going on a pilgrimage, then? When will you return? It will be harder than ever to do without you."

She replied:

> The month is passing—
> Let be the waste of time, as now
> The slow rains come;
> Tonight I shall pick me iris bulbs
> And resolution for an agitated heart.[8]

"Let us think so, and I shall soon return."

So she went and, having returned after two or three days, she had a letter from him. "I thought of visiting you at the temple, since I wanted so much to see you, but your indifference that last night was so painful that I was overcome by timidity and scarcely knew what to do. Now you probably think me indifferent to you. Actually, the last few days,"

> The days pass by,
> And though I endeavor to forget you,
> As every hour passes
> You grow that much dearer to me
> And tonight I shall admit defeat.

"I trust you understand how deep my feelings are," he concluded.

She replied with a poem.

---

[8] A second month is nearing its end. However strange, putting iris bulbs in one's sleeve was a superstitious custom supposed to bring good fortune. She pleads for some assistance from the Prince, using the pilgrimage as a way of objectifying her need.

You speak of coming loss,
But from the fact I do not see you
I feel the days creep on
As I, this while examining the creepers,
Find your vine breaks off too soon for me.

Fearing exposure as usual, he came to her in disguise.
She was certain that he would not visit her and, fatigued
as she was by her recent excursion, she was dozing. She
woke to some knocking, which soon ended. There was no
one to reprove but herself. He had heard rumors about
her behavior, and now, conjecturing that some other man
was with her, he had quietly returned home. The next
morning he sent a poem with a letter.

No one opened it;
Though I stood there waiting at your gate,
There among black pines;
It surely is a signal instance
Of what can hurt the trusting heart.

" 'Is this not what is meant by misery?' I asked myself
that and felt thoroughly wretched."
So he really came last night. How rash she had been
to fall to sleep like that! And she sent a reply.

Why was it then
That though by those black pines
The gate was shut,
You know without examination
Whether or not my heart is true?

"I very much dislike your unjust suspicion," she added.
"If only I could show you my heart . . ." That night he had
plans to visit her again, but his departure was prevented
by the conversation of numerous people. Among those
with things to say to him were the Crown Prince and the
Home Minister, so that in his effort to do nothing rash,
he allowed many days to pass by without a visit.

The rains set in. In this heavy season, there came no
bright interval, either in the weather or in her personal

affairs. She fell into an endless reverie of love. What was the case with him, and what with the world of love they had shared? There were a number of men who were attempting to interest her in them, but in spite of the fact that she gave no sympathetic thought to these gallants, numerous stories were circulating at the Court. No doubt her life could be called living at least, but she wished she could hide herself away. A letter came from the Prince. "How are you during these trying days of rain?"

> Perhaps you think
> These long spring rains are falling
> Just as they always have,
> But those that fall today are mingled
> With the tears I shed in love of you.

It was a pleasure to have news of him and to find that he had not overlooked her in this depressing season. She wrote one poem.

> I cannot tell
> That these rains are really mingled
> With your tears of love,
> But I feel within me another rain
> That knows my sorrows to the heart.

And then, turning the paper over, she added another.

> Time and rain fall on,
> And with them all I come to know
> Is increasing misery,
> Oh, that the long rain of my thought
> Would raise the waters and swallow me.[9]

"If only there were some river bank waiting for me . . ." When he read what she had written, he immediately sent a reply.

> What do you mean?
> How can you propose to throw yourself
> Into the stream?

---

[9] The poem is typical of the conceited imagistic style in the *Diary*: there are two wordplays in the original. Another poetic style in the *Diary* is that of imageless or almost imageless poems, of which the Prince's next verses provide a representative example.

You cannot think that you alone
Are subject to the anguish of man's rain.

"It is a terrible world for us all," he added.

It was the fifth of the Fifth Month, and the rains did not stop. Her recent reply showed that she had been even more depressed than usual, and he felt terribly sorry for her. When a new day dawned, with the rain falling worse than ever, he wrote, "Didn't the rain make a disturbing noise last night, though?" and more to that effect. She replied:

Throughout the night
I listened to the sound of rain
Beating on my window;
Throughout the night what was it
That filled one's listening heart?

"How strange it is that even under cover my sleeves should have grown wet," she added. He thought that, really, she was no inconsiderable person and so replied:

I as well as you
Spent the night in listening
To the sound of rain,
Wondering how the house might pass the night
While lacking eaves to husband it?

Numerous people went about noon to the Kamo River, hearing that it was nearing flood.[10] He also went to look and later wrote. "How are you just now?" he asked. "I have been out looking at the river."

If one might compare,
One would see that though the waters
Swell to fill their banks,
The deep love that wells up in my heart
Exceeds the swelling of the flood.

"Do you understand the way I feel?" he asked. She replied:

And now all the more
You will not be able to ford the banks

---

[10] Historical records for the year speak of very high waters on the 19th and 20th of the Fifth Month.

Of the swollen waters,
For the comparison prevents your visits,
Your heart a river in a deepening flood.

"Your nice words alone do me no good," she added.

Having decided to visit her, he was having his clothes incensed and shaken when Jijū, his old wet nurse, came to him. "Where is it that you are planning to go?" she inquired. "People talk about this affair of yours. The Lady is after all a nobody, of no importance. If you wish to take her under your protection, it would be all right to have her here under your care, but it is painful to see this shiftless going out at night. Especially since they say it is a place where other men are visiting. All manner of unsuitable things might come up. Everything wrong seems to begin with that Lieutenant of the Right Guards—it was he who got His Highness your late brother started on these rendezvous. What good can there be in going out for such purposes all the night? The people who go out with you probably report to the Great Lord.[11] You ought to consider that nothing in the world can be certain from one day to the next, and that his Lordship takes counsel about affairs at Court.[12] Until you know exactly what you can expect in the world, would it not be best to give up these pointless excursions?"

When he had listened to all this, he replied, "Where am I going? I am bored and want to have a little amusement, that's all. It's nothing for people to bother themselves over." He said no more. It was true that the Lady treated him with disdain, but it was not as if she were not worth his efforts. How would it be to establish her here in the

---

[11] Probably Fujiwara Michinaga (966–1027), then Minister of the Left, who became virtual dictator and who figures in *The Diary of Murasaki Shikibu* and numerous other accounts of the time. It is not clear whether the author describes an accepted reality of the supervision of Princes of the Blood in this way, or whether Jijū is meant to be using a bogeyman. Plain-speaking retainers are found in many literatures, but from her first question, Jijū can be recognized as an immemorial Japanese type in life as well as fiction.

[12] The first half of this sentence is obscure; it is also uncertain whether this is the same lord as that just mentioned. Some editors implausibly identify this one with Fujiwara Kaneie, who had died in 990. The reference is in any event to a nobleman of the highest rank.

palace? But then there would be even worse lectures to listen to. With such division in his thoughts he gave up visiting her for some time.

At last he went to see her. "It is true that I have behaved badly to you, since in spite of myself other matters have occupied me, but you must not think that I have wavered in my attachment to you. And I think that much of the fault in my not coming is yours. There are numerous people who frown upon my visiting you. And during that time when I was trying to act so cautiously, the worst thing was that so many days went past without my seeing you." His manner of speaking conveyed his fidelity to her. "Now, come with me," he urged, "if just for tonight. I know of a place where no one can observe us. We can talk at ease there and put our minds at rest." With this he had the carriage brought around, and brooking no resistance, he commandeered her into it. She rode off as if all this were happening to another person. She could not put from her mind the fear that people would hear about this, but since the night was already grown full dark there was no one who knew what had happened.

When the carriage entered the palace grounds, he had it pull up at a hall where there was no sign of anyone. He alighted. Since the moon was so bright, he said firmly, "Please get out." She stepped out without much enthusiasm. "Come, come," he said. "You can see there is no one else here. From now on let us get together in a place like this. One cannot always feel at ease at your house, because there are apt to be other men there." This and much more he said with tenderness. When it had begun to grow light, he had the carriage brought around. "I ought to accompany you home, I know,"[13] he said, "but by the time I got back it would be full daylight, and it would be very

_____

13 In the elaborately worked-out code of relations between the sexes, a high nobleman had a principal wife or consort and possibly other wives, concubines, or mistresses. He was expected to visit the woman, who commonly continued to live in property inherited matrilineally. But if the woman's rank were much lower than his, as is the case here, she might visit him or be installed in his house. The scandal that upsets Jijū is not so much the affair itself as his unseemly behavior in visiting someone of such low rank as the Lady. All this does not prevent the Lady from feeling that her going to him compromises her.

troublesome if I should be seen." So he remained behind.

All the way home she thought, "What won't people think about my going out in this distasteful way?" But when she was home and thought of the incomparably handsome figure of the Prince as they parted at dawn, she wrote him,

> Though I return,
> Sent back each time in darkness,
> There is yet one thing—
> One does not like one's being forced
> To wake when light breaks in the sky.

"How painful it was to part at dawn."
  He sent a poem in a letter.

> To wake and part
> Just as the dew falls in the morning,
> That is misery,
> But much worse yet is that dark night
> When one returns with unrequited love.[14]

"So let us not hear anything more about being forced to wake up. Since it is ominous for me to stay with you, I shall come and get you." It was painful to think that she might be going out every night, but when night fell, he came in the usual carriage. He escorted her with a "Hurry, hurry!" She was embarrassed to be spoken to in such fashion before others and got out and into the carriage thinking over and over how unpleasant it was. They went to the same place as on the previous night and there were able to talk on. The Prince's Consort believed that he had gone to visit his father, the Retired Emperor.

When the first light of morning had come, he said, "How I hate to hear the rooster crow," and he quietly entered the carriage with her and accompanied her home. All the way back he told her, "I hope we can always go like this on these occasions." "Why must we always have to be going out?" she protested. Having seen her home, he returned straightway, and in a short time his next-morning letter

---

[14] Alluding of course to the incident of misunderstanding, when he visited her only to find he could not gain entry.

FIG. 8. Ariwara Narihira
From a poem-card in the series Hyakunin Isshu.

Property of the translator

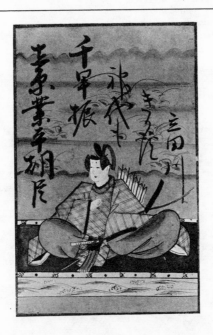

FIG. 9. A Leaf from *The Diary of Izumi Shikibu*

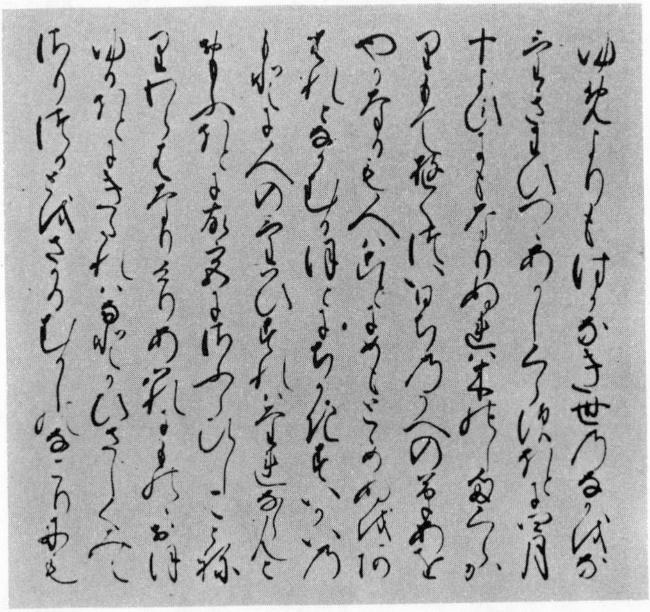

FIG. 10. The Courtyard and Western Inner Gate of a Courtly
    Mansion
*An imagined version, there
being no architectural certainty.*

Courtesy of Kadokawa Shoten

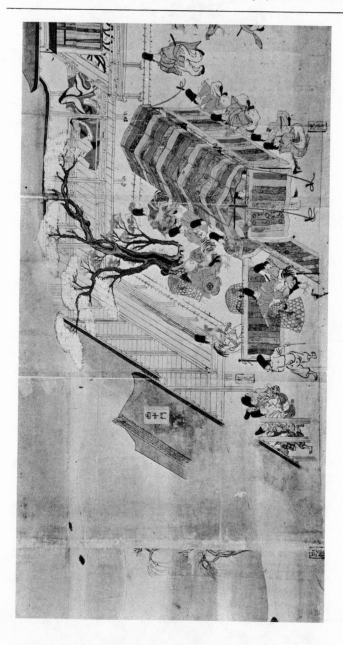

Fig. 11. Priest Nōin

From a poem-card in the series Hyakunin Isshu.

Property of the translator

Fig. 12. The Palace of Fujiwara Michinaga's Family

Reconstructed design by Ōta Seiroku, "Tōsanjō-dono no Kenkyū."
The most accurate design made, this leaves out
the Northern Chamber of the Consort for lack of
accurate information.

Courtesy of Kadokawa Shoten

Major Areas

1. Principal Chamber
2. Eastern Chamber
3. Other Chambers
4. Galleries
5. Verandahs
6. Carriage House
7. Pavilion
8. Archives

9. Household Shrine
10. Courtyards
11. Western Main Gate
12. Eastern Main Gate
13. Southern Inner Gate
14. Western Inner Gate
15. Eastern Inner Gate
16. Islands in the Garden Lake

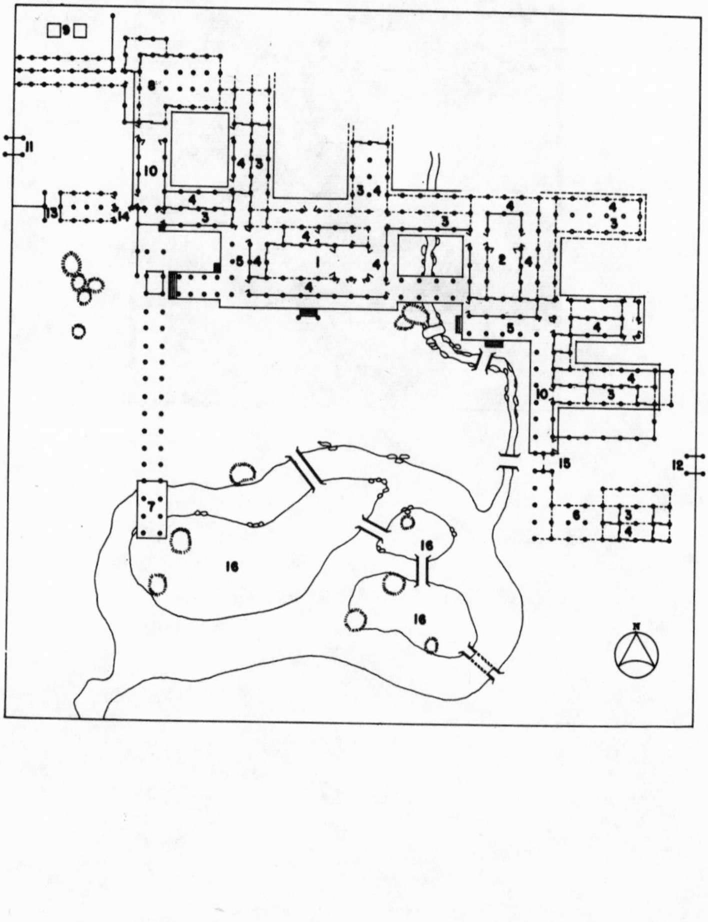

arrived. "Because that cock woke us up and parted us this morning, I have had him killed," he wrote, attaching a poem to a chicken feather.

> Though I killed him,
> It is not punishment sufficient
> For such a heinous crime—
> Not to know the occasion, to shatter
> This morning's dream with just one crow.[15]

She sent a reply.

> How bad it was,
> Yet it is I who have had to suffer—
> Morning after morning—
> The misery of being forced to hear
> The cock crow out that it is dawn.

"What unhappiness the crowing has brought me."

Two or three days later, on a night with a brilliant moon, he went out on his verandah to gaze on it. "What about it?" he wrote. "Are you looking at the moon?" And he added a poem.

> Do you feel with me
> Regret that the moon should set
> Behind the rim of hills,
> Telling our hearts of what we shared
> And sigh for as it disappears?

As she was taking more than usual pleasure from his letter, she thought how bright the moon had been in that hall of the palace. Wondering whether they might have been seen by someone after all, she replied with a poem.

> It may be as you think,
> That this moon is the same we shared
> Through that lovely night;
> But as I watch my eyes grow dim,
> My heart can scarcely tell its way.

So that while she was watching the moon alone, the new day dawned without a visit from him.

---

15 The killing of the cock is of course a polite fiction.

The next night he came again, without her hearing of his arrival. There were living in different rooms of her house numerous women of differing ranks. The carriages of their men were at the house, and when he came in his, he assumed that she was being visited by someone else.[16] He had not counted on such difficulties, but in spite of the embarrassment he did not think of ending the relationship. He sent a letter immediately on returning. "You have no doubt heard that I came for you last night. What I encountered was absolutely beyond words."

> Though I have seen
> Such wonders as the surging waves
> High upon Mount Matsu,
> The long rain that I beheld today
> Surpasses the waves beyond belief.[17]

It continued to rain. What could he mean speaking in such terms? Someone must have been putting ideas into his head. She protested.

> And now I know
> That you rise like the fickle waves
> To Mount Matsu's end,
> But who is there here resembles you,
> To ford her way across such troubled waters?[18]

For his part he could not forget the shameful experience of that night and for a long time sent no news. But a poem did come at last.

---

[16] The house no doubt contained a number of rooms or apartments where women of various ranks lived and to which, given the customs of the day, came men who were husbands or lovers or at stages between. It is this ménage that a prince of the blood encounters to his horror. Such an experience might be expected to keep him away forever. Some editors have decided that this refers to Izumi Shikibu's living with her sister and presume to know that there was one carriage and its owner's name.

[17] The poem echoes an anonymous "Eastern Song," *KKS*, XX: 1,093, an allusion suggesting the Prince accuses the Lady of infidelity. The allusion means that he suggests either, "I have known before that your establishment is a confused one, but what I saw—!" or, "I have suspected before that you were untrue, but now I know." (He cannot dismiss from his mind the other men he encountered.)

[18] She recognizes his allusion and, with a somewhat confused allegory, alludes to the same poem herself, turning the accusation of infidelity back upon him.

> I have no moment
> Free from divided thoughts of you,
>   For now I think
> Of your fickleness with resentment
> And again of you with love.

It was not as though she had nothing to say in return to such a declaration, but she felt uneasy that he might think her making excuses. So she only wrote:

> I shall not grieve
> Whether we meet or do not meet again,
>   But this I do regret,
> That a fact misunderstood
> Should break so bitterly our love.

After that news seldom came from him. She lay musing one night when the moon was shining brightly. "How I envy you,"[19] she thought, and in that state of reflection wrote the Prince.

> Looking on the moon
> I fall into a tender reverie
>   In my ruined house,
> Wondering whom I might tell of its beauty
> When I know that he would fail to come.

She gave the poem to a young bathroom maid, saying, "Take this to the Lieutenant of the Right Guards." Many people were deep in talk with the Prince at that time, however. When at last they withdrew, the Lieutenant gave him the letter. Upon reading it he at once ordered, "Have the carriage brought about as before." She was still at the edge of her chamber, looking out upon the moon. She had the blinds dropped when she heard someone enter the grounds. He came in, his appearance even more strik-ing than usual, wearing softer, ordinary dress instead of the stiff formal clothes he had always worn before. His new appearance quite took her fancy. He placed a letter

---

19 The phrase recalls a poem by Fujiwara Takamitsu (d. 994), *SIS*, VIII: 435, in which the clarity of the moon is favorably contrasted with the darkness of human life.

upon his fan and had it handed to her, saying only, "I have come myself, because your messenger returned without this." Since she had retired within her chamber, she was at an inconvenient distance for speaking and so took the note with her own fan.

He was thinking how much he wished to join her in the house. As he wandered about among the shrubbery of the garden, he recited, "Is she not like dew upon the leaves?"[20] He seemed so very attractive. Approaching her, he said, "I must go back tonight. I just came by to see if I could tell who it was that visited you the other night. I have told my people that tomorrow is a day of abstinence[21] for me, and they would think it strange if I were not at home." Since he seemed about to go, she recited a poem.

> Just for a trial,
> I could wish for rain to fall,
> To put its light to proof—
> If the moon that passes through the sky
> Would pass my house or linger here.[22]

Her figure was slighter, her bearing more youthful than he had heard people describe her, and he thought how appealing she was. "My darling . . . ," he said, and went to her for awhile and then made as to leave.

> Drawn on by the moon
> That dwells in the imperial cloudlands,
> I go against my will,
> The radiance alone is setting forth;
> My heart remains behind with you.

With that he left and afterwards she looked at the letter he had brought. It consisted of a poem.

---

[20] Alluding most appropriately to an anonymous poem, *SIS*, XII: 761, on the intimate tenderness one feels for one's beloved.

[21] He will have a *monoimi*, one of any number of ritual defilements or deliberate abstinences such as the nobility of the Heian period concerned itself with. In theory, these could keep one very nearly incapacitated, but they were commonly used as excuses—indeed all the abstinences or avoidances of ominous quarters in the *Diary* suggest some degree of convenience.

[22] Like not a few others in the *Diary*, this poem beautifully encompasses, in the original at least, the dominant imagery of two or three episodes.

You have let me know
That for my sake you gaze in reverie
Upon the moon tonight,
And therefore I have come on purpose
To see if what you say is true.[23]

What a wonderful person he was. If only he has changed his opinions about those things spoken of her by those awful people. He was thinking for his part that she was someone with whom one could hold truly refined conversation and one who could be a great consolation to him when things got tiresome. But the gossip continued. "It seems that the Minamoto Commander is visiting her. They say he's even there during the day." And others said, "The Minister of State has also been calling on her." Hearing such things said on all sides, he began to believe that she really was an abandoned woman and did not correspond with her for a considerable time.

The familiar Page called. He was on good gossiping terms with the Lady's bathmaid, and the two talked freely about the affairs of the two houses. "Is there a letter?" the maid asked.

"No letters. The other night His Highness came by, but he saw carriages at the gate and that's probably why he sends no letters. You know he has heard that he's not the only one who has been visiting the Lady."

"That's what the Page told me," the maid reported to her.

It occurred to her that although she had had no news from him for a long time—though of course she had not gone out of her way to solicit any—still, as this woman's remarks implied, there were signs from time to time that he thought of her. Surely he had decided not to break with her completely. For all that, he was obviously suspicious because of that tiresome gossip. Such thoughts made her the more miserable, and as she was asking herself what

---

[23] This poem is in response to hers on "Looking on the moon," and it comprises the letter he brought on his fan.

she had done to deserve such treatment,[24] a letter came from him.

"Recently," it began, "I have been feeling strangely ill and out of sorts, which is why you have not heard from me. Yet on those occasions when I have come by your house, I have not found things very suitable, what with those other carriages, and so have returned home, feeling myself no longer even a human being."

> Well then, so be it—
> Even if my little fisher's boat
> Starts away from shore,
> Leaving me by rowing on the offing,
> I shall not hate her for the loss.

How she detested the terrible gossip that had come to his ears! It was demeaning to do so, but for once she would seek to excuse herself with apology.

> Truly I am she,
> The fisherwoman who has lost her boat,
> Who can rely on nothing
> But the task of producing salt
> From the tide-soaked Bay of Sleeves.[25]

With that exchange of letters it was now the Seventh Month. On the seventh there were a number of poems and letters from various gallants about how the Herdboy visited the Weaver Maiden,[26] but she paid no attention to them. In the past he had always made sure these occasions did not pass by unnoticed; now it seemed that he had really given her up. Just as such thoughts were weigh-

---

[24] The last eight words render *Nazo mo kaku*, a phrase that is thought by some editors to echo an anonymous poem, *KKS*, XVIII: 934. Other echoes have also been suggested.

[25] The allegory, based on a suppressed comparison of tears and salt water, need only be mentioned; but the way in which the boat image is turned back on the Prince deserves some stress.

[26] The 7th of the Seventh Month was the Festival of Tanabata, in which the Herdboy was supposed to have his single annual meeting with the Weaver Maiden (representing the "meeting" of the stars Altair and Vega) across the River of Heaven, the Milky Way.

ing her down, there was a letter from him. She found on inspecting it that it consisted only of a poem.

> Have you not thought
> That you have become the Weaver Maiden
> Who looks in reverie
> Across the wide river plains of heaven
> For a lover who comes but once a year?

He had not forgotten her altogether. He had not let the festival pass by unnoticed, and her spirits rose. She wrote:

> So I "look in reverie";
> But I do not look upon your heavens,
> Since I know too well
> I am one who meets but detestation
> When the Herdboy ought to visit me.

When he read these verses he thought that, after all, he could not give her up.

Towards the end of the month he wrote: "It has been a long time since I heard from you. Why don't you write sometimes? You probably do not regard me with any more affection than the rest." She replied to that with a poem.

> You sleep too well
> And untroubled by any thoughts of love
> You cannot hear:
> Yet the wind that blows across the reeds
> Sends its invitation every autumn night.

He at once replied. "Oh, my dear, you think I 'sleep too well!' You know what the old poem says about 'When one is in love . . .'[27] You must not believe me indifferent."

> I shall not sleep
> If over the reeds the wind will blow
> An invitation to me,
> And it seems I should have listened
> To hear it say, "From now on, stay awake."

So it was that about two days later at dusk his carriage suddenly drew into her grounds and he alighted. He had never

---

[27] "When one is in love / One cannot even feign one sleeps," according to a poem in the *Tsurayuki Kashū* (*Zoku Kokka Taikan*, 17,753).

before come while it was still light, and it made her feel quite constrained. There was no help for it, and at loose ends as he was, he went back to his palace. She grew very apprehensive in the next day or so at not hearing so much as a sound from him and so wrote him briefly.

> The twilight falls
> Upon my heart and on the autumn days
> Passing one by one,
> Making clear how you regard me
> And how strange our meeting was.[28]

"Truly, our lot in this world . . ."[29] He responded after a time. "I have not kept in touch with you recently as I ought to have. However,"

> I cannot speak for you,
> But as for me I shall not forget,
> However time may pass,
> What it was like to meet with you
> In the evening of an autumn day.

It seemed that there really was nothing left to hold to, nothing to depend upon in just exchanging poems. For a time there was promise of consolation in the world of their love, but upon examination it brought only disappointment.

With matters in this posture, it was the Eighth Month. She decided to go to Ishiyama Temple for a week to find some relief for her drooping spirits. Just after she left, it happened to come into his mind, "How long it has been since I have been in contact with her!" He wrote a letter, but the Page said, "I called on the house yesterday, and it seems that she has gone to Ishiyama or some such place."

"Well, it is already grown dark," said the Prince. "Pre-

---

[28] Much of the predication of the poem is in the last line (which with other details echoes an anonymous poem, *KKS*, XI: 546): dusk should bring the lover, but when he grows unfaithful, it is the most miserable time of day for the waiting woman.

[29] Echoing the third line of a poem by Priest Nōin (998–1050), *SIS*, XVII: 1,104.

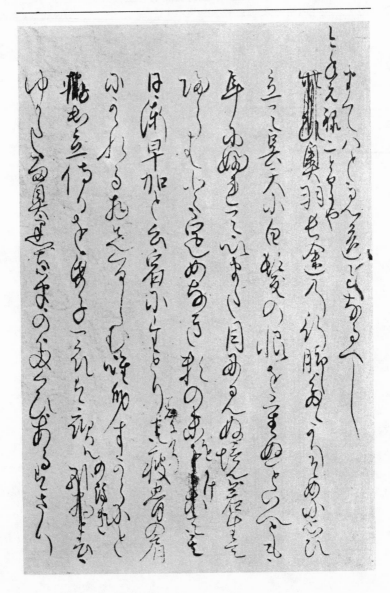

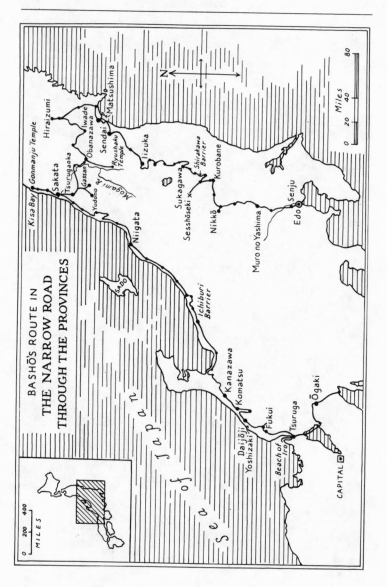

pare to set out the first thing in the morning," and he wrote
a letter which he gave to the Page.

He set off with the letter to Ishiyama but could not find
the Lady at the altar before the Buddha. She had gone off
to one side. There, longing for the familiar capital, thinking how even on this pilgrimage her affairs were so wholly
altered from what they had been, and finding herself
miserable in every way, she was praying devoutly to the
Buddha for assistance. From where she was, she looked
below the balustrade where someone seemed to have come
up. As she looked down more intently at him, it turned
out, to her astonishment, to be the familiar Page. Happy
to find him there so unexpectedly, she asked, "What brings
you here?" To this the Page responded by giving her a
letter. She opened it and read it with more than ordinary
interest.

"I appreciate the devotion that has taken you to the
temple, but why did you decide not to tell me? Of course
you may not wish to be shackled to me, but this leaving
me behind altogether is something I find terribly cruel."

> I wonder if you thought
> That today my inquiry would cross
> The Barrier of Meeting?
> Although that messenger, my heart,
> Has always beaten its way to you.[30]

"When will you be coming home?"

She felt pleasure and surprise that, although he should
ignore her when she was close at hand, he had taken such
pains to communicate with her now. She replied with
poems and a note.

> Who can it be
> That has set out to inquire for me
> Past the Meeting Barrier,
> When I thought you had forgotten
> The road to meeting by this lake?[31]

---

[30] To get from the capital to Ishiyama Temple near Lake Biwa, it was
necessary to pass Ōsaka no Seki, "the Barrier Slope of Meeting," a check-
point lying east of the capital.

[31] The first line of the original (the last of the translation) plays upon
Ōmiji/au michi, the road to Lake Biwa, or Ōmi, and the road of meeting.

"You ask when I shall return. Did I come here with no clear thought of what I was doing?"

> At a mountain temple,
> A swamp of troubles might arise,
> But when I shall return
> In misery to the capital is something
> You must tell from watching Leaving Bay.[32]

He told the Page when he had read what she had written, "I know the journey is a hardship, but you must go again." And he wrote, "Can you ask who it is that inquires? That really is saying too much."

> My message crossed
> The valley of the Meeting Barrier
> But to no avail.
> Feigning ignorance of the sender,
> You now seem glad just to forget.

"So you only give me back my question about when you return?"

> Though you may think
> The world's miseries can be shunned
> With religious solitude,
> Look at Leaving Bay on the Lake of Meeting—
> The scenery that brings you home to me.

"You know what they say, 'Think of me whenever you are miserable.' "[33]

To all that she replied simply,

> Not even the hills
> Are barrier sufficient for my tears,
> For it is they that flow,
> "Whenever I am miserable," to form
> The Lake of Meeting I desire so much.

But following this on the sheet, she added another poem.

---

[32] As the contortions of the translation may suggest, the original is highly conceited; "Leaving Bay" renders an actual place-name.

[33] From an anonymous poem, *KKS*, XIX: 1,061. It may be remarked that the allusions in the *Diary* are consistently to poems in the later books of the *Kokinshū* or of other early collections.

> My visit here
> Was just a venture that you might
>   Try to make your own;
> Or, now, if someone to good purpose
> Would call me to the capital again!

Truly, why not go visit her where she was deciding what to do? But how was he to do it? She returned meanwhile. Hearing of this, he wrote, "I thought you wished for someone to 'call me to the capital again.' Since you have come back so quickly,"

> It is astonishing,
> Your stopping in mid-journey on the path
>   Of the Buddha's Law,
> And who can it be has called you
> That to the capital you come again?

In reply she wrote only:

> I have left the hills
> Of the Buddha's Law to take my way
>   On the world's dark road,
> Coming now yet again in hope
> That we might meet if only once.

Towards the end of the month the wind blew up in a gale, bringing wet weather. She had a letter from him, just as her spirits were depressed more than ever. He exhibited his usual discrimination about the seasons so well that almost without knowing it she pardoned his recent neglect.

> Grieving always,
> And lost in a reverie of gazing
>   At the autumn sky,
> I find its scenery is like my heart
> With shattered clouds and storming wind.

She replied with a poem.

> When the autumn wind
> Blows in its usual gentle way,
>   There is cause for sadness,
> But when the whole long day is darkened,
> There are no words to speak of grief.

That seemed to him to express the nature of things exactly. But days passed as usual without his writing.

Late in the Ninth Month he was awakened by the pale light of the moon lingering in the sky at dawn. How long it had been since he was in touch with her! She was prob-ably looking out sadly on this very moon. Or was it possible that some other man was there? Nonetheless he set out with only the usual Page. When they knocked at the gate, she was lying down awake, her mind running over this and that. It was the melancholy season of autumn, and she was sunk even more deeply than ever in low spirits and was gazing out vacantly upon the world.

That was strange. Who could be knocking at this hour? With some effort, she woke one of the women sleeping in her chamber and sent her to have a man answer the gate. But he was slow to wake. Still half-drunk with sleep when at last he was roused and, bumping into this and that, he made a great clatter in his struggles. The knocking had ceased by the time he got to the gate. Whoever it was must have gone away. How embarrasing to think that her visitor would believe her lacking in sensibility on this autumn night. The caller must have been someone with a mind like her own, unable to sleep on such a night. Who indeed could it be?

By this time even the man had fully waked and, looking outside was able to report to all concerned, "There's no-body here! You just thought you heard someone. It was probably only somebody lost in the night, you stupid maids, you." And he fell right back to sleep.

Sleep was out of the question for her, however, and pres-ently the new day dawned. As she lay gazing at the thick mist blanketing the sky, the light grew brighter. She was able with this to set down on paper the feelings she had had upon being awakened at dawn. As she was finishing, the usual letter arrived from him. He had not written very much.

> Unable to wait
> Throughout the long autumn night
> Until the moon

Fades into the brightening sky at dawn,
I came home emptied of my hopes.[34]

So it had been he after all. How heartless a woman he must be thinking her, and yet more than that he had not let this particular moment pass. How akin he was, to feel so deeply the cast of the sky at dawn. In her pleasure at the discovery, she took the papers she had written that morning and, folding them together just as they were, sent them to him.

The sound of the wind—it blows through branches threatening to spare no leaves—more than ever it makes one feel the true sadness of things. When a little rain seems about to scatter in drops from a sky sheeted in clouds, then one feels that the sadness is almost too great to bear.

During the autumn
My sleeves have moldered with my weeping;
When the real drizzle
Comes with the winter to bring its sadness,
Who then will lend me sleeves for tears?[35]

Such thoughts occupy me as I sigh over my situation, but there is no one to share my feelings with. Although it is not yet the season for the late autumn drizzle, such a rain has been blown up by the cold wind, changing the very color of plants.[36] When I see them withered, caught in a heart-rending way in that wind, I think that I myself will in a moment vanish away like the dew,[37] so much do I sense in myself a fragility like that of these plants. As I look out upon them in the sway of the autumn wind, I think with anguish about my own similar life, and therefore instead of retiring within the room I lie by its outside edge, unable to sleep at all. With the people of the house all dead asleep, I my-

[34] The descriptive style of the poem earned it a place among the love poems of *SKKS*, XIII: 1,169.

[35] The drizzle, which is of course a trope for tears, is associated with late autumn and early winter. It is now the Ninth Month, October or November.

[36] Perhaps with a suggestion that the affections of the Prince have also been altered.

[37] The passage is cited by some who hold that a person other than Izumi Shikibu is author of the *Diary*, because the prose here seems to be a transformation of verses in the *Izumi Shikibu Collection*. The assumption is that this other hand either revised the passage or an earlier version of the *Diary*, changing verse to prose, or used such poems in making up the whole of the *Diary*. Of course Izumi Shikibu herself might have done the same.

self am unable to say why I remain awake, and with my eyes barely open am filled with a lazy sadness of regret, when suddenly the geese coming south cry out in flight. Can others feel this way? Certainly my feelings are too strong to be repressed.

> How many nights now
> Have I spent the hours in sadness
>   Unbroken by any sleep,
> Setting myself the single occupation
> Of listening to the voices of the geese?

Rather than just listen to the geese cry out, I pushed open the sliding outer doors and could see the moon just setting in the western sky, where it was half obscured by streamers of mist. Through such a sky the booming of the temple bell and the crow of a rooster echoed as one sound. With the past and the future coming upon me together, I cannot think to see day break this way much more often,[38] and the scene struck my feelings with such great force that there was a sweetness even in weeping.

> Not I alone—
> Others must look upon it as I do;
>   On mid-autumn nights
> The fading moon at daybreak
> Brings unrivalled feelings to the heart.[39]

If only there were now someone who would come knocking at my gate, what pleasure it would give me. But who nowadays would spend his time like this, watching dawn come?

> I would like to ask,
> Are there not others who are looking—
>   Out upon a moon
> Fading in the western sky at dawn—
> With feelings that accord with mine?[40]

It occurred to her that this might be sent to him, and just then his messenger had arrived to make it possible. He thought as he read it how beautifully she put things, and

----

[38] The syntax of the passage has been repointed from that of the texts followed and other editions.

[39] The poem is included in *ShGSS*, VII: 438.

[40] The poem is included in *ShSZS*, XIII: 1,423.

since one could imagine her still gazing at the sky, it was appropriate to send off a messenger with a reply. She was indeed still looking out and, when the messenger came with the answer, she opened it with a twinge of disappointment that he had replied too fast to have entered completely into her feelings.

> During the autumn
> My sleeve has moldered with my tears,
>   And yet you think
> That it can be your sleeve alone
> On which the drizzle falls.[41]

> Rather than think
> That one's life is but the transient dew
>   Soon formed and gone,
> Why not fully devote one's mind
> To the chrysanthemum and its long life?

> Unbroken by any sleep
> The nights pass as you listen to the geese
>   Crying in the clouds,
> And such an occupation surely comes
> From a heart determined to be sad.[42]

> Not I alone,
> But you as well have gazed in sadness,
>   Fixed upon the sky
> With a heart well matched with mine
> As the moon fades into dawn.

> Are there not others?
> I thought surely you alone would watch
>   The fading moon at dawn,
> And with such thoughts I went to you
> To find the morning desolate of hope.

As she read the poems and the line afterwards—"How I disliked that gate for refusing to open"—she thought that

---

[41] This poem, like the rest following in the series, is fully intelligible only by reference to the sequence of poems in the Lady's long pensée.

[42] The last line is obscure; among the glosses is the seemingly unlikely one (in this context) attributing wantonness to the Lady's behavior.

at least the incident had furnished him with an occasion to write.

Not long afterwards, about the end of the month, a letter came. It included an apology for not giving her more attention these days. "It's a peculiar request," he admitted, "but a woman I have been seeing recently is going off to a distant province, and I would like to send her a poem that she would find really moving. Won't you write one for me, since you are the only one who has ever written me such poems?"

He certainly seemed satisfied with himself. All the same, it would be very affected to reply, "You'll get no such poems from me." So that what she did write was, "How am I to write that kind of poem for you?" along with some verses:

> "As you now go,
> Like this autumn and our love,
>   I do not know your heart;
> But leave behind at least your image
> To sparkle in my grieving tears."

"Obviously it gives me no pleasure to compose love poems like this on your behalf." And she added afterwards, "Now truly,"

> Where does she go,
> She whom you throw off so easily?
>   But also what of me,
> Left alone in a suffering world of love
> To think of life as only passing time!

"Your poem is all that I could wish for," he wrote, "though saying so may suggest that I know all about poetry. But that 'suffering world of love' in the poem to me is over-imaginative."

> I do not mind
> That she who sets out in travel
>   Has rejected me,
> If only you at least regard me
> As the one who is your only love.

"I shall be wholly satisfied if that is the way you feel."

Soon thereafter it was the Tenth Month. About the tenth of the month he came. Because he thought the inner part of the chamber so dark as to be forbidding, they lay stretched at ease together along the outside edge of the room. He spoke to her most tenderly and lovingly, and she found it a joy to be talking with him. It was a time of the year when the moon is completely clouded over and there is a steady drizzle. The night seemed made to purpose for everything that might lend a depth to one's feelings. He looked upon her lying there in the bone-chilling cold, rapt in her thoughts. Many people spoke ill of her, but when she lay here before him like this, his heart stirred with love. In such a state of aroused feeling, he watched her relaxed posture, half in thought and half-asleep. Touching her gently, he whispered,

> There is no drizzle,
> There is no dew that falls tonight,
>   But as we lie here,
> A strange wetness glistens softly
> Upon the sleeve of the pillowing arm.[43]

She did not reply, as she lay there in the languor of thought. Only, he could see the tears falling from her eyes and sparkling in the moonlight. Looking upon her with the utmost tenderness he said, "Why don't you reply? I know that what I said was unimportant—I must have said something wrong."

"What should I say?" she asked. "My thoughts are lost in a maze of feeling, and your words have scarcely entered my ears. But this much I hope you believe—your poem about 'the sleeve of the pillowing arm' is one I will never forget. You may put me to the test on *that*." She spoke this with a sudden smile.

The next day he thought how affecting it had been to see

---

[43] Needless to say the tears of sensibility are referred to. "The sleeve of the pillowing arm" (*Tamakura no sode*) echoes through a number of the following poems and beautifully embodies much of the air of courtly romance to be found in Heian diaries, tales, and poems.

her lying like that, sunk in thought. The poor dear probably had no one she could really rely upon. It was a thought that gave pain, and he wrote, "How have you been since I left?"

She replied with a poem.

> In the morning hours,
> The sleeve of the pillowing arm
> Has quickly dried.
> It was no more than a flickering dream
> That bedewed it as you slept.

She had promised not to forget "the sleeve of the pillowing arm," and the poem gave him pleasure. He replied,

> Although you think
> That no more than a flickering dream
> Brought forth my tears,
> It is wet with sleepless yearning,
> That sleeve of the pillowing arm.

His feelings must have been taken by that wonderful night they had spent together, because from then on he showed greater consideration for her and visited her with some frequency. He would regard her posture intently, thinking her by no means the worldly-wise person she was made out to be. On the contrary,[44] she looked so helpless in the world, and he felt a pang of anguish just to look upon her. Speaking to her with great tenderness, he said, "What a depressing life you seem to lead here! It is not something I have thought through consistently—but do decide, come live with me. There are many people who spread terrible reports about you. I have come to visit you all too infrequently, and though I have not yet been seen doing so, people are saying the most painful things about my visiting you. Then there are those times when I have visited you and have been so far unable to see you that I have felt as miserable as though I were not even human.

---

[44] What follows in the original (of one of the texts followed) is fifty-seven clauses before a complete period is reached. In this translation, the unit extends through the Prince's second remarks and his return "while it was yet dark," the close of the third paragraph after this.

In fact there have been times when I have felt there was no point in continuing our relation. But since I am an old-fashioned type who feels he must be faithful, I have felt very keenly about you and of course have not given you up. It is hardly possible for me to continue to visit you in this way, since there are those who might hear about it and try to stop it. Really, let us establish a relation in which I am the moon that passes through your sky.[45] If life is tedious for you, as you often say, why not come to my place? My Consort and others are there, but you should not find it that troublesome. All the more, my position makes it very unsuitable for me to slip out at night, and I cannot live apart from the world. I also do not get much pleasure from performing religious rituals alone in the palace. I cannot help thinking that if we could have the chance of talking together, one mind and one heart, there would be comfort in it for us both."

As he spoke of these matters, it was not at all clear how she could take up so unaccustomed a life. There had been some talk, she remembered, about her going into service for His Retired Majesty. But nothing had come of that and there just was no one to help her "to the other side of the mountains"[46] when she was miserable. To spend one's life in such a state of mind is like a long dark night that will never end. There are of course many worthless men who only toy with a woman, and there had been all that terrible gossip. Was there, after all, anyone besides him for her to rely upon? Why not do what he suggested, then? Even though his Consort was there, they did live separately, and his old wet nurse seemed to perform all manner of services. One's doings would of course become widely known if one went there, but even so, who wished to be altogether hidden away? What was there to keep her from going? At least that would put an end to that tiresome story about other men visiting her.

So she replied, "What should I say? You know how my

---

[45] The sentence is variously interpreted, and the original of the words quoted said to be various poems, none of which fits the context particularly well. The interpretation followed here is that the Prince has recalled her poem, "Just for a trial," on p. 112.

[46] Echoing an anonymous poem, *KKS*, XVIII: 950.

time is spent in great uncertainty and sadness. In the past you have occasionally come as a comfort to me during those times when I was only living from one day to the next. In fact, I have had no other policy than to make known how I have waited for your visits. Perhaps you feel that the situation is just as you describe it, but even if I were to do what you suggest, wouldn't people still talk about us in ways that would distress you? I should feel all the more terrible to have my moving to your place make people think that, yes, all that gossip about us has been true."

"As for gossip," he replied, "it is rather me that people will criticize. But who will think that your situation would be one to be pitied? I shall have a place built for you completely hidden away from prying eyes and come take you to it when it is ready." With such reassurance, he departed while it was still dark.

The lattice curtain through which he had left was still up, and she lay stretched out in the cold on the verandah by herself. What should she do? Would she not be laughed at by people? With her thoughts wholly unsettled in this way, a letter came.

> Dawn was just breaking
> And dew covered the mountain path
>   As I came back;
> The sleeve of my pillowing arm
> Was wet with tears and with the dew.

The "sleeve of my pillowing arm" was a trivial matter, but it brought pleasure to see that he had not forgot it. She sent a poem in reply.

> In the early morning
> The dew settles on the roadside grasses
>   Before one's waking eyes,
> Allowing no chance for drying out
> The sleeve of my pillowing arm.

That night the moon was unusually bright, and both here and at the palace the two stayed up watching it till dawn. The next morning, while he was thinking of sending his usual letter, he asked, "Has the Page come in yet?" Her letter arrived just at that moment—she must have been startled by the extraordinary whiteness of the frost.

> Fallen everywhere,
> The frost lies too upon the sleeve
> Of the pillowing arm,
> And looking on it in the morning light,
> I see it white like hempen sleeves.[47]

That was unfortunate. Her letter had anticipated his, and he added verses to her last two to make a new poem.

> Looking on it in the morning light,
> I see it white like hempen sleeves—
> The frost that falls,
> Settling on me as I wake at dawn
> Loving her beside me.

The Page at last came in as he was speaking the verses over to himself. "What," the Page wondered, "is the matter with His Highness's disposition?"

"It's all because you didn't come soon enough that he is so angry with you," said the Usher, handing over the letter.

He went off to deliver it and told her, "Even before he had received your letter, he had sent orders for me saying, 'He still hasn't come,' and he has been most put out with me."[48]

"How bright the moon was last night," she read,

> That moon we saw
> As then we slept the night together,
> Has she seen it now?
> No news comes as the morning frost
> Settles on one who has waited out the dawn.

Now it was clear to her. He had meant to send this poem to her and the Page had spoiled his point. Pleased by discovering his intent, she replied:

---

[47] The poem employs a skillful use of *shirotae*, which is most familiar in its pillow-word form, *shirotae no*, "white hempen," for sleeves. The archaic pastoralism of hemp (or mulberry) does not describe, of course, her own clothes.

[48] The explanation is too simple, and is the Page's diplomatic way of explaining why the Prince's letter had not anticipated hers.

> The face you put on it
> Is that of one who waits in reverie
>   As the whole night passes,
> Watching without a moment's sleep
> Till the moonlit night ends with the dawn.

She spoke this over to herself and, as she was setting it down, the Page said, "His Highness is furious with me." Diverted by the situation, she added to her letter:

> I would like to see
> That as the frost soon melts away
>   Beneath the morning sun,
> So you may show some disposition
> Of melting in your mind toward him.

"He seems to be very anxious about your attitude."

"No doubt you think," he wrote, "that you beat me with your poem this morning. The fact is that I am exasperated and could murder that Page."

> It *is* a frost
> That ought to melt beneath the rays
>   Of the morning sun,
> But from the appearance of the sky
> It is unlikely soon to melt.[49]

She wrote in response. "So—you plan to kill him!"

> This Page is one
> Who appeared from time to time
>   When you failed to come.
> How can you think that from now on
> You will not say, "Go, you're spared for her."

He laughed over the joke and sent another letter.

> It is as you bid.
> Now the death sentence is removed
>   From this Page of ours,
> All because of what has been said
> By my beloved, secret wife.

---

[49] The imagery and allegory grow from the preceding poem: his anger will not soon "melt," but of course it is largely feigned.

"But," he added, "we seem to have forgot from our poetry 'the sleeve of the pillowing arm.'"

She protested to this.

> With no one knowing,
> I have invested my heart in you
> With my concealed love,
> So how is it you imagine I forget
> The sleeve of the pillowing arm?

But he insisted—

> If I resolve
> Never to speak of punishment again,
> Will you recall,
> Unbidden, and even for a little,
> The sleeve of the pillowing arm?

No news came for two or three days thereafter. What could his plans of providing her with a good place have come to? She could not get proper rest as she turned such thoughts over in her mind. As she lay here, wide awake, thinking it must be near the end of the night, there came a knocking at the gate. "What can this mean?" she wondered, but when she sent someone to inquire, it turned out to be a letter from him. This was unexpected. She was deeply touched, and murmured, "Did my heart go out to him for this?"[50] She had the shutters slid open and read his poem.

> And do you watch,
> As the minutes of the night go by,
> Where upon the hilltop
> It shines unblemished by a cloud,
> This bright moon of an autumn night?

That he should have been awake through the night, gazing at the moon and thinking of her. It moved her more deeply than usual. But since the gate had not been wholly opened, the messenger must be having a miserable wait of it. So she quickly composed the reply.

[50] Alluding to a poem by Priest Dōmyō, *GSIS*, XIV: 785. Dōmyō was a contemporary of Izumi Shikibu and may once have been her lover.

I keep awake,
Burdened with thoughts and wondering,
    "Has it not grown late?"
But in spite of failing to get sleep,
I am unable to see the moon for tears.

How easily she had given a more interesting turn to his
thoughts. How attractive she was. If only there were some
way of getting her near at hand to be able to enjoy such
exchanges all the time.

Two days later he came, his visit disguised by travel in
a woman's carriage. She was embarrassed to have him see
her, because he had never before visited her in full daylight. Yet, however unsuitable it might be, it was hardly
cause for shame. Moreover, it would be foolish to be embarrassed over a meeting by daylight, if he had definite
plans for the future. Her mind divided, she appeared before him hesitatingly. He apologized for having neglected
her recently and soon was lying at her side.

"Please decide soon," he urged, "about what I proposed
to you before. I cannot accustom myself to these furtive,
disguised visits. Because they make me so uneasy I often
fail to come here, and all this makes our relations painful."

"Whatever the case," she said, "I suppose it would be
best to do as you say. But on the other hand, you know
What is said, 'Familiarity brings indifference,'[51] and I am
confused about what to do."

"Come, come, do decide. You know they also say, 'Acquaintance renders dearer,' "[52] and with this he went out
of the room. He went to a thin place in the hedge at the
end of the garden and there broke off a lovely bough of
spindletree, its leaves just flecked with autumn color.
Thrusting it upright into the railing, he spoke a couple
of verses.

Like these leaves the words between us
Take on a truer depth of love . . .

---

[51] It is thought this may echo an anonymous poem, *KKS*, XV: 752.
[52] Alluding to a poem in *Kokin Rokujō*, VI (*Zoku Kokka Taikan*, 34,133).

She at once capped his verses.

> ... Only when you settle
> Like the all-too-transient dew,
> A moment white, and gone.

Really, she had the quickest perception of feeling.

And his appearance was particularly striking. He wore under his ordinary court dress an indescribably handsome fabric that showed at the edges of his gown. There could be no one more attractive. It even felt as if her very eyes grew amorous at the sight.

A letter came the next day. "Your behavior yesterday suggested that you found my visit in daylight disagreeable. Yet I felt an attraction, even while I suffered from your attitude." She sent a letter in reply.

> He felt that way, too—
> The ill-favored god of Kazuraki,
> So afraid of daylight
> That in his awkwardness he feared
> To build the bridge upon the Kume Road.[53]

"I was so embarrassed I scarcely knew what to do with myself," she added. An answer came from him soon afterwards.

> If the occult power
> Is in my hands to control a person
> Who to her own thoughts
> Is as awkward as the god of Kazuraki,
> Then by all means let us leave it so.

Not only did he write such things, but he came more often than before, to the great relief of the dreary tedium of her life.

---

[53] The god of Kazuraki was shy over his unhandsome appearance and his legend was a byword for those who feared to be seen by daylight. As the *Diary* shows, however, no Heian lady was comfortable in the light, and her initial attractions at least for a lover had little to do with physical appearance. We may assume that the physical charms of the Lady in the *Diary* were by no means negligible, but it is her sensibility as expressed in poetry and other responses that repeatedly brings back the Prince's wandering attention.

About this time it happened again that some undesirable men began sending her letters and even loitering about her house. She asked herself as these difficult matters arose why she did not go to him, but she could not wholly resolve to do so. She sent him a poem early one morning when the frost was particularly thick.

> So white is the frost
> That for my part there is no telling
> Where the plover stepped,
> But on the wings of your much greater bird
> Can the whiteness be so truly deep?[54]

He replied in the same vein.

> Frost does not fall
> At all upon the one who said she sleeps
> And does not see the moon,
> At least not so deeply as it falls
> Upon the wings of this your greater bird.

He came soon after dusk. "How beautiful the autumn foliage must be in the hills. Come with me," he proposed. "Let's go look at it."

"I hear the leaves are lovely—that would be nice."

But when the day came, she said, "Today I have an abstinence and cannot go out."

"That's terrible. When it is over, we must be sure to go." But that night there was an autumn storm that sounded so much stronger than usual that it threatened to strip the trees of their leaves. When she awoke she murmured, "Lacking support before the wind . . .," thinking how like the leaves her own case was. They must be all down now. What a pity to have missed them. Dawn broke upon such regrets, and with the new day came a letter from him.

> Do you spend your time
> Watching these long rains in pensive thoughts,
> Not distinguishing them
> From the slow drizzle of late autumn
> That slowly wastes this world of ours?

---

[54] The allegory is not strictly parallel and involves an echo of a folksong but, simply put, she suggests that his affection (frost on the big bird) does not match that of hers (plover).

"It is this deeper significance of the rain that is the true cause for regret."

Such thoughts affected her, too.

> What is it that brings,
> Is it the winter drizzle that brings
> This wetness to my sleeves?
> It becomes impossible to decide
> As I, too, deep in thought gaze on the rain.

"Yes," she added, "and such being the case"—

> The colored leaves
> Must have been downed by drizzle
> Falling in the night.
> If only yesterday we had gone
> To see them bright upon the hills.

Reading this, he answered with a poem.

> Of course, of course—
> But why was it that we failed to go
> To see the autumn hills?
> Still, this morning it is useless
> To waste our time with these regrets.

And he added after that,

> With such a storm
> You may think that they have gone,
> But come, let us go
> To see whether the autumn leaves
> Are fallen yet or bright upon the bough.

By way of reply she wrote:

> If we could find
> Some hilltops where the autumn leaves
> Remained forever bright,
> Then I would say with you, "Let's go,
> Looking, looking in delighted search."[55]

"What point can there be in such an excursion after they have fallen?" she added.

---

[55] In other words, she declines the invitation, which suggests that the abstinence preventing her outing earlier was some wholly imaginary, or at least convenient, affliction. She probably feared being seen.

One day not long thereafter he came to see her. She re-called poems and letters they had been exchanging. "With my recent hindrances, we have not been able to get to-gether, have we?" And she recited a poem.

> Let us hurry out;
> Row on, my Takase River boat—
> That which hindered us
> Has been left behind with rowing
> And the path has cleared among the reeds.[56]

"Haven't you forgot that you said you wouldn't go?" he asked.

> Surely we would go
> Riding in a carriage to the hills—
> What can this mean,
> This talk of a Takase River boat
> To go to see the autumn leaves?

She answered, with their exchange of verses in mind.

> If your autumn leaves
> Stay bright until we come to visit them
> Why yearn for them so much?
> But it is because they fall we love them,
> So why not launch our Takase River Boat?[57]

As darkness fell that day, he came again to her house, and because it lay in an ominous direction, he secretly took her away. It was a time when it had become necessary for him to abstain from his house for forty-five days, and so he moved to the quarters of his cousin of the third rank.[58] It

[56] Now that it is too late, she suggests a willingness for an expedition, echoing in her question and verses a poem attributed to Kakinomoto Hitomaro (fl. *ca.* 680–700) in *SIS*, XIV: 853.

[57] The last three poems and their accompanying prose have been in-terpreted in numerous ways. Whatever the specific obscurities, it seems likely that, having refused the serious invitation, the Lady continues to talk about it until it becomes a matter of shared talk and witty allusion between the lovers.

[58] The Prince is taking measures to deal with a real or convenient directional taboo (*kata-imi*), which includes both his palace and the Lady's house. It is not known certainly what historical person may be the cousin, but the third rank is a very high one and so his establishment would be fit for a prince of the blood.

was a place different from that to which he had taken her before and she accordingly said she could not bear to go to it. He took her in spite of her protests, however, and having put her into the carriage he had it drawn into a concealed place of the coach house. She was in a terrible fright, with the carriage left standing there and him gone into the building. He returned to the carriage after the people of the house had gone to sleep and there spoke to her at length about his love for her. But there were various low servants roaming about the area. Their familiar Lieutenant of the Guards did his best with the Page to shield them from the men, while for his part he spoke to her with great intimacy, regretting that in the past he had treated her so indifferently. Yet such explanation should not have been necessary.

He took her home as soon as the sky began to grow light and returned to his cousin's at once, "Before anyone is awake," as he put it. In the morning his poem came.

> I know too well
> The lonely succession of waking dreams,
> But now at early day
> I feel awakened from a dreamland
> Seen as we lay together in the night.

Her reply showed no liking for the circumstances of their meeting.

> Since our first night
> I have not been able to fathom
> What would become of me,
> But I had never pictured to myself
> Traveling in sleep throughout the night.

However, it just would not do, in view of all the considerate kindness he was showering on her, to show a hard heart and indifferent face. But did that mean that she should go to him, then? There were those close to her who cautioned her against the step, but she paid no attention to them. As miserable as she was anyhow, she might as well yield to fate. It certainly had not been her aim all this time to be part of his household. What she had most wished to do was retire from the world altogether to the fastness of a mountain temple,[59] although if the problems of the world were to trouble her even there, she would scarcely know what to do. People were no doubt thinking, and saying, that there was not enough religion in her to take orders. It did seem that it would be best to go to his palace[60] and try there to make her way in the world as well as possible. With his favor near at hand, she would be able to see to the interests of her relatives better and to insure the future of her daughter from the past relationship. Such a tumble of thoughts led her on, and she came to hope that until she had moved no embarrassing stories would reach his ears. Once she was under his protection, he would understand, he would dismiss gossip about her. Then it would be possible to have the servants say, "The Lady is not at home," when importunate letters came, and there would never be a need to send replies.

There was a letter from him. What she discovered in it was: "I was a great fool to trust in you." He wrote just a bit more, quoting, "I shall not know that woman anymore."[61] Suddenly her heart felt crushed. Everything had gone against her. Preposterous stories about her were circulating, and anyhow, what was to be done about baseless gossip? It was quite clear that his letter was in earnest. Now that some hint of her intent of moving to his palace must have got abroad, she could expect to be made a fool of by people who thought he despised her. It was so dejecting that she could not rouse herself to say anything in reply. As she remained silent, ashamed that he should have believed such gossip once again, he took the silence to mean embarrassment over the gossip itself, and so he wrote her, "Why do you not reply? I must have been right about those rumors. How quickly your heart can change! People had said many things, but I had always thought that they could

---

[59] An echo of part of an anonymous poem, *KKS*, XVIII: 952.

[60] Another interpretation is the opposite—that she will stay where she is —but that conflicts with the opening of the paragraph.

[61] One interpretation holds there is an echo of *KKS*, I: 42, another that there is one of *KKS*, XII: 630.

not be true. I had told myself that 'If two people really are in love / Then what does it matter what is said?' "[62]

There was some relief in reading that. But she wished to know just how the gossip had affected him. She wrote, "If it is true that you feel that way,"

> This very moment
> I wish that you would come to me;
> How dear you are,
> But since there is my reputation,
> Is it right for me to go to you?

To that he replied,

> So it is with you;
> You have worried about the issue
> Of your reputation,
> But it seems your circumspection
> Depends upon the man who is with you.

"All this fuss over your reputation infuriates me," he insisted.

In spite of his gibes, he must have known how she was suffering—but that did not take away their pain. "This really is too much to bear," she wrote. "I wish that somehow you could see me as I really am." His answer to this indicated divided thoughts.

> Although I thought,
> "I will regard her with no suspicion
> And no bitterness at all,"
> I have not been able to align
> My feeling with my thinking heart.

She also replied with a poem.

> Do not abate
> Any of the resentment of your heart,
> Now that the one
> In whom my trust was total
> Should cast his doubts on even me.[63]

---

[62] Echoing a poem by Lady Ise (fl. 935) in *Kokin Rokujō*, IV (*Zoku Kokka Taikan*, 32,960).

[63] The logic of the poem is not wholly clear. One reading is that it

Even as she was composing this, dusk fell and he came. "You know how people have been talking about you," he told her. "Although I told them it was impossible, I still wrote that letter. If you can find it in you to think all those things unsaid, then, come on, move into my palace." After speaking on in such fashion he returned home at dawn. He wrote very frequently thereafter about what he had proposed, but he found it difficult to visit her.

It was a day when the wind and the rain blew fiercely against the house. There was no news from him. There were few people in the building at all, and it was even sadder to think that he did not sympathize with the sadness she felt at the low sighing of the wind. Just after dusk she composed a poem.

> How painful it is,
> To be separated by the blight of frost;
>   For while the autumn wind
> Still blew so sadly through the reeds,
> The sound was promise you would come.

A letter came from him just as her poem was being sent off. "I have been deeply concerned, wondering how you have responded to the frightful howling of this gale."

> What must you feel
> As you listen to the tempest storming,
>   And with only me
> To inquire about you in that house
> Cut off by frost from all the world?

"How sad it is to have to try to cheer you with sympathy." It was interesting that he had after all sent to inquire in this way. He said that because of an ominous direction he had had to change his residence and had now gone to a place that others did not know about. She went—the usual carriage had come, and after the recent past, what he said

---

is a call even for resentment, that being a species, or sign, of interest and even love. Another holds that she returns suspicion to him. But it seems rather that she is saying that if the Prince, whom she had wholly relied upon, suspects her, then she may as well submit to any suffering.

had now its appeal. It now seemed all the more desirable to move to his palace, especially after they had spent a few days together, talking in a perfectly free way from morning to night, finding at last some solid happiness to replace the unspecifiable melancholy of the past. But when the ominous period was over, she returned home, only to find that today, more than ever before, parting had left her with an insatiable longing for him, and in the confused state of her passion she wrote him, scarcely knowing what she was doing.

> In an idle moment
> I have counted up the sum today
> Of my weeks and years,
> And yesterday alone of all those days
> Has been untouched by yearning care.

When he saw this, he was deeply touched. "I feel that way, too."

> We have passed the time
> Without a single care to trouble us.
> Can there be no way
> To make today as satisfying
> As such a yesterday and day before?

"That is what I want. But there seems to be little chance of my getting it. Really, make up your mind to move in with me." But it is not so easy to decide such a matter and, what with her vacillating this way and that, sunk in desultory thought, day after day passed by.

There was now nothing left of the brilliantly colored leaves on the various trees in her garden. In a sky bright with the clear cold, the sun gradually set in the west. As its last sad rays went dim, the scene led as usual to a poem,

> Of course I know
> That you are there to bring me
> Ease for a lonely heart,
> Yet as I wait the sky at evening
> Has a sadness difficult to bear,[64]

---

[64] Again, dusk is invested with a symbolic import as the time of the lover's visit and, failing that, of great sadness to the forlorn woman.

which brought a reply:

> Without exception,
> Everyone finds the sky at evening
> Arouses his sad thoughts,
> But it is you who more than others
> Feel the anguish of such an hour.

"Thinking that way, I can't tell you how much I value you. If only I could go to you at once!"

He sent by to inquire, "How are you getting on just now?" so early the next morning that the frost was still heavy. A reply was called for.

> The world can give
> Nothing that causes greater grieving
> Than to be awakened
> After a night of waiting by the frost,
> Bringing the morning with its fall.

This was sent as part of their exchange of poems, and as usual he wrote back very feelingly, including a poem.

> To feel alone.
> Thoughts of a love as deep as mine
> Is no use at all.
> I hope that your heart is stirring
> With the love that stirs in mine.

She had to reply.

> So you may wish,
> But since we cannot divide us,
> Saying you are you
> And claiming that I am only I,
> How can we speak of different hearts?

About this time she fell ill of a cold, nothing of an alarming nature but enough to put her off color and enough, too, to get him to inquire about her with some frequency. Just as everything was improving, he wrote, "What is your condition now?"

"I am rather better. Of course it is sinful to think, 'Oh, to live just a little longer.' And yet"—

My firm resolution
When you broke off your visits
    Was to break my life,
But the fragile jewel-thread of my soul
Has twisted stronger in its love for you.[65]

"You have no idea," he replied, "how that pleases me. Nothing could make me happier."

How could it break,
That fragile jewel-thread of your soul,
    When the vows we made
Created a relationship between us
Bound up by our two loving hearts?

The year drew to its close about the time they exchanged those poems. Would spring not be a good time to move to his palace? It was toward the beginning of the eleventh month, on a day of heavy snowfall, that a letter came from him:

The snow we see
Is that familiar in its falling
    Since the age of the gods,
But though it is something known so long,
It falls today in rarest loveliness.

She wrote in reply:

When each winter comes,
I say, "the first snow fall is here,"
    And think it wonderful,
But there is no wonder in the way the years
Fall on me as the snowfalls claim my gaze.

One day followed the next with exchanges of such casual verses.

A letter came. "I am afraid that I have not been in touch

---

[65] Court poets often play upon the image of the jewel-thread of the soul, treating it as a physical image and, as in this poem and the next, often use numerous "associated words" (*engo*)—thread, jewels, break, twist, binding up, and so on.

with you. I had thought to come tonight, but it seems there is this party for composing Chinese verse." She responded,

> For lack of time
> You cannot come to visit me.
> Let me go, then, to you:
> What I seek is knowledge of the way
> That leads to Chinese verse and you.

Finding the idea behind the verses of interest, he wrote:

> By all means come,
> Come inquiring at my house;
> I will teach the way
> That leads to Chinese verse and me
> And gain another chance with you.

One morning when the frost was unusually thick, he wrote asking, "How do you think it looks?" She could answer that.

> On these cold nights
> I count their numbers like the snipe
> Ruffling each his feathers.
> How many mornings have I awakened,
> Alone, to see the frost upon the ground?[66]

And again, because the rain fell so heavily about this time—

> These are days indeed
> When now the heavy rain comes down,
> And now, it seems, the snow,
> And days when your affection wanes
> Like nights awakened by the morning frost.

That night he came, and along with his usual tender words, he said, "Wouldn't you be upset after coming to my palace if I deserted the place to go into orders?" The most alarming thoughts arose when one heard him speak so despondently. Plunged into such despair, she fell to weeping. All this time rain mingled with sleet was slowly falling outside. It was no night for sleeping, and he pledged his faith

---

[66] Echoing an anonymous poem, *KKS*, XV: 761. As the succession of seasonal images and of human activities in the poems of this episode shows, the purpose of this section is to give a sense of the passage of time.

not only in this life but in that to come. He spoke so tenderly, his words flowing forth. She resolved within herself
to go to his palace—and yet, what if he should enter orders? What other course would there be but to follow his
example? The thought was so depressing she could not
speak. When he saw the tears flowing so heavily, he recited
three verses.

> Spending our time
> Worrying about what is to come,
> Throughout the night . . .

She completed the poem.

> . . . Our sadness has brought our tears
> To fall as if they were the rain.

His dejected appearance did not suggest that it would be
possible to rely upon him completely. He left for home as
dawn was breaking.

It was by no means certain just what expectations of the
future might be held out by a move to the palace, but there
would be some solace to loneliness. In spite of that attraction, however, the prospects he had opened the night before could only leave one wondering what to do and me-
andering in confused thought. She sent him a letter.

> What was said last night
> Was of a sadness far too great
> To think reality.
> I wish to treat it as a dream
> To be forgotten as we wake.

"That is what I want—but how can we make it a dream?"
She added a poem of explanation.

> For all the bonds
> That we pledged to hold us close,
> The world you offer me
> Is one whose nature is unresolved
> And makes me unsure of what you mean.[67]

---

[67] Throughout this period of the *Diary*, the Lady cannot put from her
mind his suggestion that he might enter orders, leaving her without sup-

"I regret it a great deal."

When he saw the letter, he at once wrote, "I had hoped to anticipate you in writing."

> I wish you to think
> That that was not reality at all—
> Not those unhappy things
> We spoke of in the dream we saw
> While sleeping out our night.

"Did you really take my talk seriously? You are too easily put out."

> What is unresolved
> Is rather the length of time we live,
> But the promises
> That we exchanged remain as changeless
> As the boughs of Sumiyoshi pines.[68]

"My darling, I shall not trouble you again with worries about the future. But it is painful not to be able to tell another what is really in one's heart."

After that it was a matter of thinking miserably and sighing constantly. If only it were possible to move to the palace without any delay. A letter came from him about midday. It contained an old poem.[69]

> How dear it is,
> The flowering pink I hope to see
> Blossoming like this
> Upon the fence of my secluded home—
> You, the dearest flower of the land.

---

port. The *Diary*, like numerous poems outside it, shows Izumi Shikibu torn between the attractions of the world and the repose of the religious life. The tension was widespread in the age, and many took orders or first vows on reaching a suitable age.

[68] Sumiyoshi was famous for its unchanging pines and auspicious quality; cf. *Tosa Nikki*, pp. 82–83, above, or the anonymous poem, *KKS*, XVIII: 905.

[69] The exchange of this and the next poem is the cleverest in the *Diary*. The Prince's letter consists of an anonymous poem quoted from the *KKS*, XIV: 695, applied significantly to their situation. Recognizing as much, and finding that the decision to move which she has been delaying so long is being thrust upon her, the Lady skillfully quotes back another poem from the *Ise Monogatari*, 146, suggesting that he come to her. His recognition of her intent is signaled in his good-humored response.

"He must be beside himself," she said aloud, "what with these sudden changes of disposition." She challenged him with another old poem.

> If I am so dear,
> Then why do you not come to visit me?
> Mighty they may be,
> The gods, but their injunctions
> Do not prohibit lovers' nights.

He could not help chuckling when he read the poem she sent. Recently he had been devoting himself to study of the sûtras, and so it was that he wrote:

> The meeting of lovers
> Is a way of life that does no damage
> To the virtues of the gods,
> But I who study here the Buddha's way
> Ought not to leave my mat to visit you.

If that were the case, she could say:

> If things stand so,
> Then it is I who should set out to you.
> Allow me the request
> That there upon the Buddha's prayer mat
> You make room for me to learn his Law.

Some time passed with such exchanges. Then, after a heavy snowfall, he sent some kind of branch, still laden with snow, and a poem attached to it.

> As the snow falls,
> Even before the spring the leaves
> Of every kind of tree
> Without exception blossom forth
> With the white flowers of the plum.

And in return, she wrote,

> It seemed to me
> That already the plum had flowered,
> But when I broke a spray,
> The snow fell down upon the hand,
> Appearing just like falling flowers.

Early the next morning he sent a poem.

> So dear you are
> That I passed the winter night
>   With no sleep at all.
> Without my dear one I spread out
> My gown until the break of dawn.[70]

She wrote in reply, "You may say so, but . . ."

> During the winter night
> It seemed my tears froze on my eyelids,
>   Closing them with ice,
> And I lay alone until the dawn
> Opened on my painful night and eyes.

As the days passed, such poems brought some relief to the burden of loneliness. But what a meaningless life!

What he was thinking was not clear, but about this time he began to send the most depressing letters. "For all I can see, I do not have much longer in this world."

That called for reply.

> You intend to leave
> A world having woes as numerous
>   As the Chinese bamboo joints,
> But what of me left behind to ponder
> Our ancient tale of love and all alone?

He soon responded.

> With troubles as many
> As the many joints of Chinese bamboo
>   In this world of ours,
> I for one would not stay in it
> Even for just a little while.

He had at his disposal a place unknown to others. He knew that because it was unfamiliar to her it would be somewhat embarrassing for her to go to. And for his part, too, it would be somewhat awkward to have it spoken of.

---

[70] Lovers were spoken of as sleeping, pillowed in each other's arms, on or under their adjoining spread-out gowns. To "spread out one side" (*katashiku*), or sleep alone, was the loneliest thing for a lover.

FIG. 16. The Prostitutes Tell of Their Plight
From a six-fold screen illustrating the diary,
with text and poems by the haikai *poet Yosa Buson.*
By permission of Hasegawa Kichirō, owner, and by courtesy
of Chikuma Shobō

For all that, he would lead the way himself. He came on the eighteenth night of the Twelfth Month, just as the moon was at its brightest. He spoke his usual "Let's go together," and she thought that this was just for tonight and so boarded the carriage unattended.

"It might be better if you took one of your women," he said, "in case we want to spend some time at our ease." This was not what he usually said. Or could it be that he intended to establish her there? They left with one of her women. It certainly was not the usual place but one that gave the impression that it was intended to house someone with a servant or two.

So that *was* what he intended. So she was there. How much better to have no fuss over her arrival. Let people ask later, "When did she come here?" When it was light she sent for her comb boxes and such personal things.

Because he was expected momentarily in her new quarters, the lattice was set in due order. There was no question of her feeling afraid, but sensing the constraint in the air, he said, "Let's go over to the northern quarter.[71] Here we are too close to the edge of the palace and so cannot really relax." Having said this,[72] he dropped the lattice that enclosed them in the room. Listening unobserved to what was going on outside, he said, "During the day various of my servants and those who serve my father the Retired Emperor throng about here. What about it—would you like to live forever in a place like this? You may find that life with me in the palace looks better from a distance than near at hand. It is not all that pleasant." Having said this and heard her say, "I almost think so, too," he laughed and went on. "Really, at night and at other times when I am away, take care. You cannot tell what worthless sort may be peeking about. You ought to move after a little while to the quarter

---

[71] As the *Diary* suggests, this is the section of a palace or house in which the principal wife, the "consort," lived by right, so giving her her title as *kita no kata*, or "the one of the northern quarter."

[72] What follows, to the next "Having said this," is not in the best manuscript. The repetition of the phrase probably led a copyist to skip the material between, and the section in question is therefore given here as part of the *Diary*.

of the Chief Lady-in-waiting.[73] Unlike other parts of the palace, that is one where people are not always coming and going. Do live there."

Two days later, observing his manifest preparations for a move to the northern side, the people of the palace were astonished and took the matter to the Consort, who thought that things had been intolerable enough without this. The Lady was no one for a prince to fuss over. And to think that he had told her nothing about this. His bringing her here secretly was a sign that he was infatuated with the woman. The Consort's great displeasure, so much beyond her usual irritation, kept him from visiting the northern quarters for some time. After hearing a certain number of tiresome remarks from the people of the palace, and pitying the Lady's isolation, he stayed for a time with her.

The Consort was distressed. "It appears that there are various recent matters that you might discuss with me. Why is it that you don't? You do not need to be afraid that I would try to dissuade you from anything . . . You know that this really does not show proper human consideration for me. People will ridicule me and I shall be endlessly humiliated." She fell to weeping.

"What need is there for you to be concerned," he replied, "if I bring someone into my service here? With you so angry over the matter, Chūjō and the other ladies-in-waiting are behaving most spitefully towards me. It is not at all pleasant, and I have therefore brought this Lady here to tend to my hair and such things. There is no reason why you should not call upon her services, too." This by no means suited the Consort, but she said nothing.

A number of days passed in this way. She became more and more accustomed to service in the palace, occupying a place beside him during the daytime and seeing to it that his hair and numerous other personal needs were attended to. He found more and more responsibilities for her. There was scarcely a moment of separation from his side, and his

---

[73] The person is called Senji, an appellation which the editors associate with the highest-ranking ladies-in-waiting of the houses of princes or other high nobility. As this suggests, lower ranks waited upon higher, and the Lady's service to the Prince is therefore not to be thought demeaning in any way.

visits to the Consort's quarters grew less frequent. The Consort could only grieve constantly.

Another year began,[74] and on New Year's Day a very large group of the nobility gathered at the palace before going to the celebrations of homage to the Retired Emperor. The Prince appeared among the throng. What a pleasure it was to look upon him—he was so youthful and handsome, so far above the common run of men. His appearance was such as to make her feel almost ashamed of herself. The ladies serving the Consort went along the edge of their quarters to observe the scene. "Come on, now," one of them said, "don't look at the men, look at *her*." There was a bustle to get a peek. But for all their poking holes in the blinds they had little luck in getting a glimpse. The Prince returned after dark, when the official celebrations were completed. The higher ranks of the nobility saw him home and, making up a party, had a concert performed. Amid such splendid happenings she thought back upon the life of boredom at her house.

During this period of her attendance upon him, he heard that there were unpleasant stories circulating among the more menial servants. That, he felt, was unworthy of the Consort and, regarding her behavior to be distinctly displeasing, he visited her even less often than before. The Lady felt very ill at ease, but as she wondered what might be done to make things easier, she concluded that there was really no other course open to her than attending him and following his wishes.

The elder sister of the Consort was in attendance as a wife of the Crown Prince.[75] At a time when she was back at their father's palace, she wrote to the Consort: "Can it really be true what people are saying these days? If so, it is an insult which touches even me. Do come back home

---

[74] Given the autobiographical interpretation of the *Diary*, the new year is 1004.

[75] The elder sister is thought to be Princess Seishi, daughter of Fujiwara Naritoki. The Crown Prince was Okisada, brother of Atsumichi by the same mother, and later Emperor Sanjō. A crown prince would have what was in effect a consort (*kita no kata*) as well as other "wives" or ladies.

some night when your moving could not be seen." When the Consort read this, it seemed to her that things had been intolerable enough without her being made the object of general gossip. She became very unhappy and replied to her sister. "Thank you for your letter," she wrote. "Our position as women is never what it should be, and lately I have had some painful things to put up with. If I could visit you for just a little while, it would give me the chance to see you and your children, and that would provide a much needed lift for my spirits. Do send a carriage by to pick me up. I, too, am anxious to hear no more of these distasteful stories."[76] Having written in this vein, the Consort made the necessary arrangements for departure.

After she had had her rooms put thoroughly in order, the Consort told her waiting-ladies, "I am thinking of staying for a time at my home. The reason is that at the moment it is not at all pleasant for me here, and I think that my presence must be disagreeable to His Highness as well, since he no longer visits these quarters." When she had said so much, the ladies burst forth in a chatter.

"Have you ever heard of anything so shameful? Everybody is outraged by His Highness now!"

"Not only did that woman come here, but His Highness went out himself and fetched her here!"

"She has everything more luxurious than you ever saw."

"She's there in a chamber of her own. They say that even during the daytime he visits her three or four times."

"Your Highness really ought to punish the Prince properly for once. He never has paid you the attention he should."[77]

The Consort's feelings were tried more than ever by such malignant talk. Things could go as they would—living near him, the very sight or sound of him would be distasteful. Since she had written her sister asking for carriages to be sent straight off, before long her brothers came

---

[76] Another reading for the sentence is, "Even if I were to make a request of the Prince (for transportation), he probably would pay no attention to me." This follows the preceding sentence more smoothly, but the verb of the second clause is the humble one for the self and so inappropriate for the Prince.

[77] The sentence is very elliptical in the original, and although the interpretation here grows from the comments of the editors, some other person than the Prince, and some action other than that given, may be meant.

to the palace, saying, "We have come to escort the Princess." And so she decided at last upon departure.[78]

It came to the attention of the Lady Senji that the wet nurse of the Consort was putting various rooms in order in the northern quarter, and so she spoke to the Prince: "With all this bustle, it appears that Her Highness is going to move to her sister's. Word of this will reach the Crown Prince. Your Highness ought to go to her and prevent her leaving."

To observe such commotion made her feel sorry for the Consort. Yet even though she felt sorry for the dislocation of the household, it was not her rôle to say anything, and she merely listened to what went on. It would be good to get out of such an unpleasant situation, even if for a little while. But that would create problems at least as bad, and so she resolved just to stay in attendance. Yet she expected never to see the end of trouble.

He went in to see the Consort, who regarded him calmly enough. "Is it true," he asked, "that you are going as I have heard to your sister's palace? Why didn't you say anything to me about providing you with carriages?"

"No, there is no need," the Consort replied. "Because they are sending for me from the other palace." And having said this, she would say no more.

What has been given above is not the wording of the letter of the Prince's Consort or of what was spoken by the ladies in the palace; it is rather what the author has imagined. So my manuscript says.[79]

---

[78] The sentence is particularly obscure and is variously interpreted. ". . . thought . . . do so" is about what the original says, but who thought what in response to whom or what is unclear.

[79] The comment on the *Diary* has raised numerous interpretations. One holds it to be evidence that Izumi Shikibu did not compose the *Diary*; others hold that it means she composed all up to the italicized portion, or that one copyist composed the first italicized sentence and that another added the last words. Yet another, remarking on the frequency with which works are so concluded in older Japanese literature, holds the ending to be a conventional technique used by the original author. But it may also be that the *Diary* grew, in smaller or larger part, from material by Izumi Shikibu and that the note therefore distinguishes the reality of the earlier portions of the *Diary*—which are matters verifiable by the Lady or easily imagined by her—from matters concluding the *Diary*, which involve speculation about what was written and said by people out of her ken.

The Narrow Road Through the Provinces

(*Oku no Hosomichi*)

by Matsuo Bashō

The Narrow Road
Through the Provinces

The months and days are the wayfarers of the centuries,[1] and as yet another year comes round, it, too, turns traveler. Sailors whose lives float away as they labor on boats, horsemen who encounter old age as they draw the horse around once more by the bit, they also spend their days in travel and make their home in wayfaring. Over the centuries many famous men have met death on the way; and I, too, though I do not know what year it began, have long yielded to the wind like a loosened cloud and, unable to give up my wandering desires, have taken my way along the coast. Last autumn,[2] as I cleaned the old cobwebs from my dilapidated house by the riverside,[3] I found that the year had suddenly drawn to its close. As the sky of the new year filled with the haze of spring, I thought of going beyond the Shirakawa Barrier,[4] and so possessed was I by some peripatetic urge that I thought I had an invitation from the god of travelers himself and so became unable to settle down to anything. I mended my underpants, re-corded my rain hat, and took three bits of moxa cautery. I could not put from my mind how lovely the moon must be at Matsushima. I disposed of my property and moved to Sampū's villa.[5]

> My old grasshut,
> Lived in now by another generation,
> Is decked out with dolls.

---

[1] Echoing the Preface of *Ch'un yeh yen yen t'ao li tu*, by Li Po (701–762).

[2] Early autumn of 1688, after returning from travel to Suma and Sarashina.

[3] Referring to a residence of some months at his house along the Sumida River in Edo, now Tokyo.

[4] Alluding to a poem by Priest Nōin (998–1050), *GSIS*, IX: 518, and possibly also to a verse by Li Po.

[5] Sampū (1648–1733), proper surname Sugiyama, was a follower of Bashō in poetry.

This and the rest of the first eight stanzas of a *haikai*[6] I left posted on a pillar of my cottage.

The twenty-seventh of the Third Month, the sky at dawn was hazed over, and observing the pale soft light of the moon as it faded from the sky,[7] I looked beyond to where the peak of Mount Fuji rose dimly in the sky, and then nearer at hand from Ueno to Yanaka, wondering when I would again see these cherry blossoms. I felt a heaviness of heart. Everyone with whom I was on close terms assembled the night before I was to leave and saw me off on the boat. As I was landing at a place called Senju, my heart was burdened by the thought of the many miles stretching ahead, and my tears fell over such a parting on the illusory path of this world.

> With spring leaving,
> The birds cry out regret, the fish
> Have tears in their eyes.

That poem marked the beginning of the pilgrimage, but it was difficult to set forth. There were all my friends gathered to see me off and apparently prepared to stand there till they saw the last of my back vanish down the road.

This year, that is to say 1689, the thought suddenly entered my head to go on an aimless wandering through distant provinces. I knew that the sufferings of travel are said to bring a fall of frost to one's head, like snow from a Chinese sky; still, there were places I had heard of but had not yet seen. To live long enough to arrive back home was a happiness I could not rely upon. With thoughts of such kinds occupying my mind, I found that at last I had made my way to the post station of Sōka. The pack of things on my bony, thin shoulders was giving me pain. Setting out with nothing but what I could bear myself, I carried a stout

---

[6] It was common to think of the first eight stanzas of a *haikai* (as also in the earlier linked verse, *renga*), as comprising the opening unit. They were commonly written on one fold of a sheet of paper.

[7] Echoing a passage from the chapter, "Hahakigi" in *The Tale of Genji* (trans. Waley, I, ii).

paper raincoat to keep out the chill at night, a cotton kimono, raingear, something in the way of ink and brush—
and various things given me as farewell presents and therefore difficult to dispose of. It was the traveler's dilemma,
knowing them a hindrance and unable to throw them away.

We paid homage at the shrine of the god of Muro no
Yashima. Sora,[8] who accompanied me on the journey, explained: "The god enshrined here is called the Flower
Blooming Princess and is the same as the deity of Sengen
Shrine on Mount Fuji. She was called Muro no Yashima
after giving birth to Lord Hohodemi when she had entered
into a house without doors and set herself on fire to prove
his divinity.[9] It is because of such a background that poets
associate smoke with this place." It is also forbidden here
to eat the *konoshiro* fish, which smells when overheated,
but almost everybody knows the outlines of such stories.

The thirtieth, we are stopping at a place in the foothills
of Mount Nikkō. The owner of the inn approached us.
"People call me Buddha Gozaemon," he said. "I am honest
in all my dealings—people will tell you as much—so spend
a night of your travels at ease in my little inn." Had the
Buddha appeared, then, in temporary form in this corrupt
world of ours, perhaps to save one like myself, a mendicant
or pilgrim in the habit of an itinerant priest? If one examined the innkeeper's conduct closely, one would discover no calculation or worldliness, only a thoroughly honest man. He was a kind such as the Confucian *Analects*
speak of, with a strength of will and rugged honesty close
to the ideal virtue—an admirable purity of disposition.

The first of the Fourth Month, we worshiped at the
shrine on this mountain. Long ago the characters used for

---

[8] Sora (1650–1711), surname Iwanami (later Kawai), was a disciple
of Bashō, accompanied him on at least one other journey, and kept a
record of the present journey, *The Diary of Sora*. The differences between
Sora's detailed factual account and Bashō's reveal how substantially Bashō
altered actual events in the interests of art.

[9] A story in the *Kojiki* says that the princess announced her pregnancy
after but one night with her husband. To prove it his, she gave birth
safely in a closed, burning room; hence the child's name, Hohodemi,
"Visible by Firelight." See *Kojiki*, ed. Kurano Kenji (Tokyo, 1958), *Nihon
Koten Bungaku Taikei*, pp. 133–135. For another version, see *Nihongi*,
trans. W. G. Aston (London, 1956), pp. 70–73.

Mount Nikkō were the "Nikō" meaning "Double Rough," but when the Great Teacher Kūkai set up a temple here, he changed the name to "Nikkō" or "Sun's Radiance." It is not clear whether or not he had foreseen what would be a thousand years later, but now the light of this radiant place reaches everywhere, extending the benefit of the temple to the last corner of the country, assisting all four classes[10] in the peaceable and prosperous conduct of their affairs. More might be said, but feeling hesitant at such a place, I put aside my brush.

> As all begins afresh,
> On the green leaves, on the young leaves
> The brightness of the sun.

It is strange to see the late spring haze draping Blackhair Mountain, and patches of white snow lingering whitely, also belying its name. As Sora put it:

> Shaving off the old,
> Here beneath Blackhair Mountain,
> We don summer clothes.[11]

Sora belongs to the Kawai clan, and his given name is Sōgorō. His house was so close to mine that its eaves touched the fronds of my Banana Plant Hut,[12] and he helps me with my kitchen work. Now he is with me on this trip, taking pleasure in being able to look on Matsushima and Kisa Bay, willing to endure the hardships of travel. On the morning we set out, he took the tonsure, put on a priest's black robes and changed the characters for his given name, Sōgo, from those with a worldly meaning to others with a religious significance. It was in connection with these matters that he wrote his poem on Blackhair Mountain. Since there is the deeper religious significance to the changing of clothes, that last line has special significance.

---

[10] The four classes are those of feudal Japan: soldiers, farmers, artisans, and merchants. Bashō obliquely praises the shogunate.

[11] The verses play on "shaving" and the name of the mountain. They also refer to the change from winter to summer clothes on the 1st of the Fourth Month, the actual date of the visit to Nikkō. In addition, Sora alludes to his change to religious garb that Bashō mentions later on.

[12] The description is of course heightened. Bashō took his poetic name from his Banana Plant Hut (Bashō-an).

Climbing the mountainside for half a mile or so up from the shrine, we came upon a waterfall. It flew down a hundred feet or more from cavernous boulders at the peak to hundreds of rocks below, gathering at last into a fresh, clear pool. Because one can enter a hollow in the rocks and see the cascade from behind, it is called Rearview Falls.

> For a little while,
> Hidden in the hermitage of the falls,
> Starting summer seclusion.[13]

Having an acquaintance at a place called Kurobane in the Nasu area, I cut across the plain from Nikkō, seeking to get straight over. As we walked on, we could just make out a village ahead in the distance, when rain began to fall and the day grew dark. We hired lodging for the night at a farmhouse, and at dawn the next day we once again set off across the plain. We came upon an untethered horse grazing. A man was cutting hay nearby, and when we asked for help, we discovered that he was not a person without human feeling, even though he had been coarsened by his work in the fields.

"What can I do?" he asked, implying that he could not leave his work. "On the other hand, the paths on this plain are a network of routes, and a traveler who does not know his way is sure to get lost. You can't let that happen. Take the horse as far as he will carry you and then send him back."

His two young children came running along as guides, though following the horse. One was a girl who told us her name was Kasane. Thinking it an elegant name he had not heard before, Sora wrote:

> Pretty Kasane,
> Or the eightfold maidenflower,
> Is what it must mean.[14]

---

[13] Bashō alludes to the practice priests sometimes followed of secluding themselves in a room for thirty days of summer hermit life.

[14] The maidenflower is a kind of wild pink and a traditional symbol for Japanese girls or women (see *The Diary of Izumi Shikibu*, above, p. 146). Sora treats "Kasane" to mean something like "multifoliate."

Coming at last to a village, we wedged some money for the use of a horse into an opening in the saddle and sent it back.

In Kurobane we visited the place of a man called, I think, Jōbōji, who was officer in charge of the fief in the lord's absence. Although he had no expectation of our visit, he seemed to take great pleasure in seeing us and talked with us for days and nights together. His younger brother, with the pen name Tōsui, came to keep us constant company. He also took us to his own house and got us invitations to the houses of relatives. A number of days passed by in this fashion, and on one of them we made an excursion to the outskirts of Kurobane. We took a look at the former dog-shooting grounds and made our way through the well-known bamboo thicket of Nasu to the tomb of Lady Tamamo.[15] From there we paid a visit to the Hachiman Shrine. When we were told that the time Nasu no Yoichi transfixed the fan with an arrow at the Battle of Yashima he had prayed for success to this Hachiman of his clan, we were impressed all the more. We returned to Tōsui's house as darkness fell.

Kōmyōji, a temple for Shugen ascetics, is not far from his house. We paid a visit to it, worshiping in the Founder's Hall.

> I pray I may fill
> Clogs as worthy as the Founder's:
> Crossing far summer hills.

Beyond Ungan Temple in this province are the remains of the hermitage of my religious instructor, Bucchō Oshō.[16] He once sent me a poem:

> The grass thatched hut
> Does not measure even five feet
> In height and width;

---

[15] It will be observed how military matters, and archery in particular, unify the Kurobane episode. On Lady Tamamo, see n. 18. Hachiman is the god of war. The famous story of Yoichi's remarkable archery can be found in *The Tale of the Heike* and many other versions. A member of the Minamoto forces, he pierced with an arrow from great range the rising sun emblem on a fan attached by the Taira enemy to the mast of a ship in the Inland Sea. The Battle of Yashima was a climax in the Gempei Wars of the twelfth century.

[16] Bucchō (1644–1716) was a Zen Priest.

I might knock it into bundles
If it did not save me from the rains.

"I wrote these two stanzas on a rock near the hut, using
a piece of pine charcoal," he added.

A crowd of people decided on their own to come with
me when I spoke of going back for a look at the remains,
walking off with my staff to Ungan Temple. There was a
large number of young people among them who led us
a merry time until, without realizing it, we had arrived at
the foothill below the temple. The mountains appeared to
extend a great distance beyond, and the paths through
the valleys grew ever fainter in the distance. The pines
and cedars clustered darkly together, the mosses beneath
them dripping with water. Even the summer sky, which
ought to have been sunny clear through, was cold to look
upon. At a place outside the gate to the temple grounds,
there is a spot from which one can see all ten famous views.
We stood there for a time by a bridge, and then crossed it,
entering into the main gate.

Now we wondered where we might find traces of
Buccho's hermitage and so scaled the mountain behind the
temple, discovering the tiny hut built on stones and back-
ing upon a cave. Its appearance brought to mind the
deathly isolation of Priest Yuan Miao and the hut on the
rocks of Priest Fa Yun.[17]

> The noisy woodpecker, too,
> Spares the hut still standing in silence
> In summer-clustered trees.

I left that patchwork of verses on a beam.

From Kurobane we go to Sesshōseki. Jōbōji had lent me
a horse, and the man leading it said to me, "Please write
down a poem for me." He seemed to me to have surpris-
ingly refined tastes for a groom, so I wrote:

> Cutting across the moor,
> Draw still the horse you lead along—
> Hear the wood thrush again.

---

[17] The Sung Priest Yuan Miao immured himself for fifteen years, and
the Liang Bishop Fa Yun was associated with the isolated temple he had
built on rocks.

Sesshōseki turned out to be slightly off toward the loom of the mountains from the Hot Springs of Nasu.[18] The stone itself retains its poisonous properties, and such insects as bees and butterflies lay dead around it so thickly that we could scarcely see the sand underneath. The willow that Priest Saigyō wrote of, "Rippling in the pure spring water,"[19] is at the village of Ashino, where it still grows on the ridge between two paddyfields. The magistrate of this area had sometimes said to me, "I wish that I could show you that willow of Saigyō's," and I had wondered just where it might be. And today I have actually come and stood in its shade.

> Planted, the single field—
> All too soon I must leave the shade
> Of Saigyō's willow.

As the restless days of travel were piling up, we came at last to the Shirakawa Barrier, and my unsettled feelings gave way to calm. It surpasses what Taira Kanemori implied when he wrote from here, "If I could but convey / To those at home some hint of this."[20] One of the three barriers in the northeastern provinces, Shirakawa has always had special appeal to poets and other men of letters. The richly leaved branches were the more precious because the autumn wind heard by Priest Nōin still lingers in the ears, and an image remains of its famous scarlet autumn leaves. The white hydrangeas are pale as linen and the wild rose blossoms vie with them for whiteness, the whole giving the feeling of snow in its coloring. Fuji-

---

[18] The name Sesshōseki means "life-quelling stone," taken from the stone described. Poisonous gases no doubt related to the geological formations producing the hot springs made the stone seem mortal. The stone was said to be a metamorphosis of Lady Tamamo (see n. 15), a fox in human guise who successfully ensnared the attentions of Emperor Konoe (r. 1141–1155) till exposed by a diviner. She then fled to the north and ended as this poisonous stone.

[19] Alluding to a poem by Priest Saigyō (1118–1190), *SKKS*, III: 262, made famous by reference to it in a *nō* play. Saigyō is the poet most often mentioned or alluded to in *The Narrow Road*, the next, Priest Nōin. Both were itinerant poets like Bashō.

[20] Quoting from a poem by Kanemori (d. 990), *SIS*, VI: 339.

wara Kiyosuke[21] has set down how a man came to this barrier and tidied his headgear before he would cross it.

> The white hydrangeas
> Enough to deck the head with fancy dress
> For crossing the barrier.
>
> —SORA

In such fashion we passed through, proceeding till we forded the Abukuma River. On the left, Mount Aizu towered, and on the right lay the villages Iwaki, Sōma, and Miharu, which were divided by hills from Hitachi and Shimotsuke Provinces. We passed Kagenuma, but since the sky was clouded, we missed the chance to see the reflections in its waters. At the posting town of Sukagawa we visited Tōkyū,[22] and we lingered on there for four or five days. When we met him, he asked, "How was it crossing the Shirakawa Barrier?"

"The hardships of our long journey," I answered, "had left us exhausted and feeling oppressed. Added to that there was the almost overwhelming beauty of the area, the associations with men of former times, and what had been written about it long ago. There was so much to take in that I was able to write but little verse."

> Here they begin,
> The celebrated places of the provinces,
> With a song of the fields.

"I only wrote that, thinking that it would be a pity to cross the Shirakawa Barrier without writing something."

Tōkyū responded by adding a second unit to my verses, Sora the third. After a time we had written three sets of *haikai*.

In a nook near this post station there is a great chestnut tree. A priest who has turned his back upon the world

---

21 The passage is a tissue of allusion. Bashō echoes in succession poems by Priest Nōin, *GSIS*, IX: 518; by Minamoto Yorimasa (1104–1180) on the leaves, *SZS*, VI: 364; by Oe no Sadashige (dates unknown) on the appearance of snow, *SGSIS*, VI: 492; and by Fujiwara Kiyosuke (1104–1177), who set down the story in his *Fukuro Sōshi* about one Taketa Kuniyuki.

22 Tōkyū, or Sagara Izaemon (1638–1715), probably met Bashō during residence in Edo.

lives in its shade. Was not that the kind of life Saigyō described in remote mountains, where one just picked up horse chestnuts from the ground? The thought brought a tranquility of spirit with it, and I jotted down the things that follow.

> *The character for "chestnut" is made up of "west" written above "tree." It therefore suggests the Western Paradise and recalls that during his lifetime the Bodhisattva Gyōgi made up his staffs or pillars entirely from this wood.*

To which I added,

> It is a common flower
> That the worldly think not worth their note,
> Chestnut at the hermit's eaves.[23]

Just twelve miles from Tōkyū's house, and removed some distance from the Hiwada post station, is Asaka Hill. It is not far from the road in a largely marshy countryside. The time was at hand for cutting that kind of iris I had heard called "blue flag," and accordingly I asked the people of the area, "Which plant is it that they call 'blue flag?'" I asked a number of people, but none of them could say. As I went about the marshes, inquiring everywhere, with "blue flags, blue flags" on my lips, the sun had started to glide down toward the mountain rim before I was aware. Turning right at Nihonmatsu, we had a quick look at the cave of Kurozuka and walked on to spend the night at Fukushima.

The next morning we inquired after the clothes-printing stone of Shinobu. We found the hamlet to be a small village lying beneath the rise of the hills. The stone itself is half buried in the ground. The village children came to us to tell the story of the stone.

"Long ago," they said, "it was at the top of the hill. But the farmers were so upset by the way visitors to it trampled

---

[23] The poem is typical in a number of ways. It refers to a humble flower, and displays a characteristic mingling of description and symbolism. Also, like many in *The Narrow Road*, it was used as an initial stanza or *hokku* for successive linkings with stanzas by Sora and others.

their grain, that they had the stone brought down here into the valley. It lies on its side with the printing surface down." It is possible that the story deserves some credit.

> Planting the rice sprouts,
> Busy hands recall the ancient dyeing
> On the Shinobu print-stone.

We crossed the river at Tsukinowa Ford and emerged in a post town called Se no Ue. Three and a half miles farther on, just to the left of the hills, there is a site recalling Vice-Governor Satō.[24] Having heard that the hamlet of Iizuka was in the vicinity of Sabano, we walked on inquiring everywhere. For all our questions, we came at last to a hill called Maruyama, the site of the vice governor's palace. When people told us of the grand gate that had stood at the foot of the hill, the image of the past led me to tears. At an old temple nearby there remain the graves of the whole Satō household, and standing between those of the two brave young wives, I wiped my eyes. They may have been women, but they had left a name for bravery to the world. There is a famous Chinese monument that made all visitors weep, but we need not seek so far for such a stone. Upon entering the temple to ask for tea, we were told that the sword of Yoshitsune and the pannier of Benkei were kept there as treasures.[25]

> The pannier and sword:
> Use them to decorate the Boys' Festival
> Along with carp streamers.[26]

That happened on the first of the Fifth Month.

---

[24] Satō Motoharu died fighting in the area in 1189 on behalf of the doomed cause of Yoshitsune (see next footnote).

[25] The story of Minamoto Yoshitsune and his strong faithful companion, Priest Benkei, is one of the most romantic narratives of Japanese chivalry. After achieving great things in battle, Yoshitsune was said to have been hounded down by troops of his jealous brother, the shogun Yoritomo, and to have died by his own hand in 1189 at the age of thirty. Since Sora's *Diary* says explicitly that they did not enter the temple, Bashō's artistic heightening can easily be glimpsed.

[26] Bashō characteristically deflates some of the air of romance by relating the heroic symbols to the cloth or paper carp flown on poles, one for each son of the house, on the 5th of the Fifth Month.

From there we went on to Iizuka for lodging. It is a place with hot springs, and so we took accommodation at a place offering such bathing. What we discovered was a dirt-floored room with rice mats spread out. Such a hovel had little appeal. Since there was no lamp, either, we had to rely upon the faint light of the sunken hearth to prepare our bedclothes and get to bed. As night came on, thunder rumbled and rain came down in a torrent, leaking from the roof above our beds. To add to it, we were attacked by fleas and mosquitoes. I was unable to sleep and had an attack of colic. I thought that I was about to go under. The short night of the season was at last over, and once again we set out on our travels. The distress of the night still weighed upon me, however, and I felt very low. We engaged a horse and with it we got to the post station of Kōri.

It is not a very reassuring state of affairs to have this illness while the road we must take lies vague and far ahead. Our tour is a pilgrimage through remote back country. I thought of the lack of stability in human affairs and of resigning myself to leaving my body behind in a forsaken area. The thought that I would die halfway on my journey seemed to me the will of heaven, and my spirits revived. In my new mood I stepped along jauntily, and one might say that—as we came to Ōkido in Date—I was dotty.

We passed through the castle towns of Abumizuri and Shiroishi. We had come to the Kasajima Territory and therefore inquired of people where we might find the grave of Fujiwara Sanekata.[27] "The hamlet you can see dimly off to the right," we were told, "is called Minowa, and beyond that lies Kasajima. There you can still find the Kasajima Shrine of the god of travelers and the pampas grass that was a keepsake to Priest Saigyō."[28] The rains of

---

[27] Sanekata, a poet and provincial governor, died in 998 while living in exile from the capital. Bashō feels sympathy and kinship.

[28] Alluding to Saigyō's poem on Sanekata, *SKKS,* VIII: 793, regretting that Sanekata remains only a name in the world, with only withered pampas grass a reminder of him.

the Fifth Month had set in, however, leaving the side roads all but impassable, and in my weakened condition it was best just to pass through the country, only looking from a distance upon Minowa and Kasajima. The suggestion of raincoats and rainhats[29] was altogether appropriate to this rainy season, and so I wrote:

> Yes, Kasajima—
> Over what foul roads does it lie
> Beneath summer rains?

We stopped overnight at Iwanuma.

The following morning we went to see the pine of Take-kuma—and, truly, it wakes you up, as the legend says. The roots of a single tree divide near the top of the soil into trunks, so retaining the shape that men wrote of long ago. One cannot help recalling Priest Nōin and his poem.[30] Perhaps it was because, so long ago, the man newly arrived as governor of Mutsu Province had had the pines cut down for piling under the Natori River bridge that when Priest Nōin came here on his second visit he should write, "No trace remains, / Not this time, of the famous pine . . ." They told us there that the pines have often been cut down and replanted, but now they look as if their age has been guarded a millennium, and they are truly a splendid stand. There are the verses by Kyōhaku.[31]

> You late cherry blossoms,
> Do not forget to show Bashō the pine
> Of far Takekuma.

To answer such a parting present given as we left Edo:

---

[29] The *mino-* of Minowa means a straw raincoat, and the *kasa-* of Kasajima suggests in this context a sedge rainhat.

[30] Nōin's poem (*GSIS*, XVIII: 1,043), echoed later by Bashō, runs:
> No trace remains,
> Not this time, of the famous pine
> That grew at Takekuma—
> Have ten centuries slipped away
> Before I came to look again?

[31] Kyōhaku (d. 1696) was a disciple of Bashō.

> The cherry blossoms
> Have yielded after three moons' passage
> To these two pines.[32]

We crossed Natori River and entered Sendai. It was the
fourth of the Fifth Month, the day for decking houses with
iris leaves. We located an inn and stayed over for four
or five days. There is a painter named Kaemon[33] living
here. I had heard that he was a person of great sensibility
and so sought him out. "The famous old places," he told
me, "are grown quite obscure. For some time I have been
trying to ferret them out." He undertook to be our guide
for a day. Miyagi Moor was overgrown with bush clover
and so gave rich promise of autumn scenery. At other
places with poetic associations—Tamada, Yokono, and
Tsutsujigaoka—the pony grass was in full flower. We went
into a pinewoods so thick that the rays of the sun could
not filter through, and learned that its name was "Under
the Trees." Even long ago, the extraordinarily heavy dews
of the place led a poet to exclaim, "Companions of your
lord, / Tell His Highness, 'Wear your rainhat!' "[34] The day
at last grew dark as we paid our homage at Yakushi
Temple, Tenjin Shrine, and such places. Kaemon had
given me maps he had sketched of Matsushima, Shiogama,
and other famous places in the area, and he revealed himself to be the discriminating person he is by presenting
me, as a parting gift, two pairs of walking sandals corded
with iris-blue thongs.

> The purple irises
> Are bound henceforth to my feet—
> Thongs of straw sandals.

Following the route marked on the maps Kaemon had
given us, we found along the narrow road to the north that

---

[32] Both the months and Bashō have passed along. The play on two and
three recalls a poem, GSIS, XVIII: 1,042, saying that if you ask the people
in the capital about the two pines of Takekuma, they will turn you off
with talk of three moons.

[33] Kitano Kaemon (d. 1746) was also a *haikai* poet. The irises with
which the paragraph begins and ends were associated with the Boys'
Festival of the 5th of the Fifth Month and with the Sendai area.

[34] From an Eastern Song, KKS, XX: 1,091. Some Eastern Songs were
from this area.

the sedge of the ten-stranded mat did indeed exist.[35] They say that even now ten-stranded sedge mats are presented annually to the lord of the Sendai fief.

The stone monument of Tsubo is at Taga Castle in Ichikawa Village.

The monument is over six feet high and just about three feet wide. Its surface is so covered with moss that one can only make out its inscription by the depressions. It tells of distances to the four corners of the country. There is also: "This castle was built in 724 by Lord Ōno Azumabito,[36] provincial state secretary and military commander, and restored in 762 by Lord Emi Asakari,[37] who was similarly a commander entrusted with pacifying the area, and also counselor and governor of the Eastern Provinces. The first day of the Twelfth Month." That would be in the reign of Emperor Shōmu.

From long ago the monument has been an adornment of verse and the subject of numerous stories. Ours is a world in which even mountains crumble with time, rivers change their courses, and roads go in altered routes. Stones disappear beneath the surface of the earth, great trees wither away, and saplings take their place. There are seldom any certain vestiges of what has been. Yet in this place there are wholly trustworthy memorials of events a millennium ago and, as I stand here looking upon them with my own eyes, I have the feeling of having actually seen what motivated men in ancient times. Such an experience is a benefit of wayfaring, and rejoicing over the gift of life, I forgot about the rigors of travel and was overcome even to tears.

We inquired afterwards about the Tama River in Noda and the Stone of Oki. At the famous Sue no Matsuyama,[38] a temple has been built with the same name rendered in

---

[35] The full phrase is a poetic expression for sedge. The sentence also refers to the road from which Bashō fashioned his title.

[36] Lord Ōno went to the province with Fujiwara Umakai (d. 737).

[37] Asakari was executed with his father after rebelling in 762.

[38] The Stone of Oki and Sue no Matsuyama are celebrated in numerous poems; see, for example, *The Diary of Izumi Shikibu*, p. 110, above.

Chinese fashion—Matsushōzan. Graves dot the intervals between the pines of the woods. The most intimate promises of lovers, made never to change,[39] have their outcome in these graves, and the thought made time seem yet crueler, just as the vesper bell sounded from Shiogama. The sky from which the summer rain had been falling cleared somewhat, and in the faint glowing of the moon over the water in the early dark, the form of Magaki Isle seemed near at hand. The little boats of the fishermen row in together, and from the babble of voices as they divide their catch, one can well understand the meaning of the old poet who wrote, "How sad the hands upon the net lines," and feel the touching sorrow of the scene.[40] That night I heard blind minstrels strumming their *biwa* lutes and chanting their north-country ballads. The instruments are not those used to accompany the military ballads, nor yet those used for the military ballad drama.[41] They make an artless, back-country rhythm above which the reciters raise their voices, and though recitation at one's pillow side is not very restful, it was still a triumph that such an accomplishment should have survived in the provinces.

Early the next morning we paid homage to Myōjin Shrine in Shiogama. This shrine was restored by the lord of the province[42] and now has a main building with magnificent sturdy pillars and a splendid painted ceiling. Its stone steps rise high aloft, and from above the brightness of the morning sun sparkles on the vermilion lacquer of its fence. In this unparadisiacal back country, the virtues of the gods have led to the building of such splendid shrines. It is a very precious feature of our national traditions. In front of the main shrine building there are votive lanterns, and on the front lid of one of them is

---

[39] An allusion to a passage in *The Song of Everlasting Remorse* (*Ch'ang hên ko*) by Po Chü-i (772–846), long one of the most popular Chinese poems in Japan as well as China.

[40] Echoing an Eastern Song, *KKS*, XX: 1,088. The original meant, "What charm in hands upon the net lines," but as Bashō's context makes clear, the meaning of *kanashi* had changed in some six or seven centuries.

[41] That is, a style different from those for reciting the *Heike Monogatari* and the *kōwakamai*.

[42] The lord was the powerful Date Masamune (1565–1636), who patronized a number of arts and who founded the shrine in 1607.

written, "Presented in 1187 by Izumi Saburō."[43] It was remarkable how vividly an image from five centuries ago took shape before me there. He was a brave man, a soldier loyal and filial, whose fame is alive to this day and earns him the admiration of everyone. It was written long ago: "We should bend our efforts to stay on the Way and hold to the grand principles of loyalty. So doing, we shall be accompanied by honor."[44]

The day was close to noon. Hiring a boat, we set out for Matsushima.[45] The distance is about five miles, but we soon landed at Ojima Beach.

What one can say about the place is sure to have little novelty, but Matsushima is the finest beauty spot of Japan and for it there is no need to feel ashamed of a comparison with Lake Tung-t'ing or the West Lake at Hangchow, the best that China can offer. The sea comes in from the southeast and over the years has beaten out an inlet over six miles around, and within the arc the tide comes in an eagre as it does at Che-chiang. There were islands beyond counting, some tall ones pointing each its finger toward heaven, and other low ones crawling on their bellies across the sea. Some islands are piled up in two layers, others in three; some on the left stand aloof from each other, others join hands on the right. Some look as if they were children being carried on the back, yet others as if they were being hugged—in the manner in which parents or grandparents fondle their young ones. The needles of the pines are a rich green; the sprays of the trees are blown in a whirl by the sea winds, and yet their lovely twisted forms seem to have been assumed of their own accord. The deep attraction of the place is that of

---

43 Izumi Saburō, i.e., Fujiwara Tadahira (d. 1189) was the only one of the three sons of Hidehira (see n. 52, below) who followed their promise to him to remain faithful to the ill-starred Yoshitsune.

44 This echoes a Chinese classic, but which one is a matter much disputed.

45 Matsushima is one of the great beauty spots of Japan, an island off the coast from Sendai. Bashō's account is no doubt the best known of writings of visits to the island.

the loveliest face made lovelier.[46] It must have been the special care of the god of hills, Ōyamatsumi, in the remote past of the mighty gods. And who is there that could paint or describe the handiwork of Zōka, the demiurge of heaven and earth?

The island coastline of Ojima juts from the main body of land, an island looking like a peninsula. One can still see the site of the detached temple of the Zen Priest Ungo, along with such other things as the stone he sat upon for meditation.[47] In the shade of the pines there were also one or two priests who had renounced the world, leading the lives of hermits in their grass-thatched huts, above which rose the thin smoke of fires built of pine cones or fallen needles. Of course I do not know them, but their life is appealing. As I approached them, the moon rose, sparkling upon the sea, creating a loveliness different from that in daylight. We went back to the inlet and looked for lodging. Our room was in the upper of two storeys, and we opened our window, enjoying our traveler's sleep in the freshest of breezes, borne upon us with the strangest feeling of delicacy. Sora wrote a poem.

> Here at Matsushima,
> O wood thrush, the plumage of cranes
> Would add to your song.

I decided to be silent as a poet in such a place, but though I intended to go to sleep, I could not. When I left my old hut to set out on this trip, Sodō gave me a Chinese poem on Matsushima and Hara Anteki gave me his *waka* on Matsugaura.[48] Opening my pilgrim's knapsack, I took out these poems for my companions that night. I also had the opening verses by Sampū and those by Dakushi.[49]

The eleventh we worshiped at Zuigan Temple. Long

---

[46] Echoing Su Tung-p'o (1036–1101), *Yin hu-shang ch'u ch'ing hou yü.*

[47] Priest Ungo (1582–1658) had gone from the capital (now Kyoto) to a temple supported by the rich Date daimiate. The site must have been abandoned not long before Bashō's visit.

[48] Yamaguchi Sodō (1642–1716) was a *haikai* poet and Hara Anteki (dates unknown) a physician and *tanka* poet.

[49] For Sampū, see n. 5, above; the dates of Nakagawa Dakushi are unknown.

ago the first of its thirty-two abbots, Makabe Heishirō, went to T'ang China after taking orders and on his return founded this temple.[50] When the Zen Priest Ungo later came here, his great virtue enabled him to attain comprehensive understanding of Buddhist teaching, and he set about to refurbish the chief Zen temples, to put gold leaf on their walls and to decorate their altars till they shone with dazzling brightness. The temple is become a great center of piety and learning—a temple which makes people think that the Buddha's Paradise was achieved here. I wondered where the temple of Kenbutsu might be.

On the twelfth we took Hiraizumi as our aim. With memories of places like the Pine of Anewa or the Bridge of Odae celebrated in many poems, we walked over roads where there were but few tracks, roads used only by hunters and grass-cutters, and so became unable to say which direction lay where, losing our way completely but at last coming out in the harbor town of Ishinomaki. I looked across the waters at Mount Kinka, which Yakamochi had written about for Emperor Shōmu as the blossoming of gold flowers,[51] and I saw in the harbor hundreds of the little boats that ply along the coast, while in the village the houses lay so close as to struggle with each other for room, and above them the smoke from cooking fires spiraled up over an area as far as the eye could see. We had come here with no intention of visiting at all, and now when we sought to rent lodgings we found that there was no one who let them. At last we found a pitiful little place to spend the night, and the next morning we set out once again on random travel over unknown roads. We

---

[50] Makabe Heishirō was a prominent priest during the Kamakura period (i.e., *ca.* 1185–1382). Bashō has him going to T'ang rather than Sung China and has changed the date of this paragraph from the 9th, and the next from the 10th. He mistakes the founder and gets thirty-two generations of abbots from no source known today. The Kenbutsu Bashō wonders about later in the paragraph flourished *ca.* 1107–1123.

[51] Alluding to a poem by Ōtomo Yakamochi (718–785), *MYS*, XVIII: 4,097.

walked along the embankment of the Kitakami River, getting glimpses from afar of places celebrated in verse— the Sode Ford, the Pasture of Obachi, and the Reed Plain of Mano. Trudging on a road along a lengthy expanse of marshy ground, we found that the countryside weighed heavily upon our feelings. We came to a place called Toima and there spent the night. At last, the next day, we arrived in Hiraizumi. The distance we had covered was more than forty-five miles.

The splendors of the three generations of Hiraizumi[52] now comprise the briefest of dreams, and of the grand façade there are only faint remains stretching out for two and a half miles. Hidehira's castle is now leveled to overgrown fields, and of all the splendors of his past, only Mount Kinkei retains its form. Climbing up to the high ramparts of what had been Yoshitsune's stronghold, one can see below the Kitakami River flowing in a wide stream from the south. The Koromo River pours past the site of loyal Izumi Saburō's castle, then beneath these ramparts, and at last into the Kitakami. The old relics of others like Yasuhira are to be found separated to the west at Koromo Barrier, which controlled the southern approach and probably was meant to protect the area against incursions by the northern tribesmen. Yoshitsune and his brave adherents took refuge in this citadel, but the most famous names claim the world only a little while, and now the level grass covers their traces. What Tu Fu wrote[53] came to my mind—

> The country crumbles, but mountains and rivers endure;
> A late spring visits the castle, replacing it with
> > green grasses . . .

and sitting down on my pilgrim's hat I wept over the ruins of time.

---

[52] The rebellious but splendid court at Hiraizumi was established by Fujiwara Kiyohira (d. 1126) in 1094. Its next two generations were those of his descendants: Motohira (d. 1157) and Hidehira (d. 1187). Hidehira's eldest son, Yasuhira (d. 1189), disregarded his father's charge to support Yoshitsune. His betrayal led the ruthless Yoritomo in turn to destroy him and Hiraizumi in 1189. See n. 43, above.

[53] Bashō adapts lines from "A Spring View" (*Ch'un wang*) by the T'ang poet, Tu Fu (712–770).

The summer grasses:
The high bravery of men-at-arms,
The vestiges of dream.

And by Sora:

The white hydrangeas—
One can see in them Kanefusa,
Brave when white-haired.[54]

I saw at last with astonishment the wonders of Chūson Temple, of which I had heard before. In one hall there are statues of the three great generations of Hiraizumi, in the other their coffins and three statues of the Buddha. But the seven sacred treasures had been scattered, the jeweled door was broken by the wind, and the gilt pillars were moldered by frost and snow. Yet a place that ought long since to have been utterly reduced and left level under the turf has been enclosed not long ago, and with the roof retiled it withstands the wind and the rain. It is preserved for a time as a remembrance of the past.

The brightness lasts
Undimmed by ages of summer rain:
The Temple of Light.

We looked for a moment upon the road to the north, where it ran obscurely off toward Nambu, and went our way, stopping that night at Iwade. We had decided to pass by Ogurozaki and Mizunoojima, following a route past Narugo Hot Springs to the Barrier of Shitomae, then crossing the mountains to Dewa Province. Because there are so few travelers on this route, the barrier guards treated us with great suspicion, and we were let through only after much delay. We struggled up a steep mountain trail and, finding that the day had grown dark, stumbled into the house of a provincial border guard and asked to be let lodging for the night. A fierce rainstorm howled for

---

[54] One of the heroes of the Yoshitsune saga, Kanefusa showed great bravery when Yoshitsune and his family met destruction at Hiraizumi. See *Gikeiki*, vii and viii.

three days, keeping us in those worthless lodgings in the
mountains.

> Fleas and lice,
> And the sound of horses pissing
> Disturb my pillow.

Our host told us that high mountains separated this
area from Dewa and that since the roads were not at all
clearly defined we would do best to make the crossing
with a guide. "By all means," I told him, and the person
he found for us turned out to be a most reliable-looking
young man with a short curved sword at his waist and a
live-oak staff. I thought to myself, "We will surely run
into trouble today," and followed close after him, overcome with fright. As our host had warned us, we had to
struggle over high, heavily forested mountains, where not
a single birdsong was to be heard. It was so dark beneath
the trees and so thick with leafy growth that we might
have been journeying by night. And as Tu Fu wrote,
"Whirlwinds of dust blow down from the clouds, bringing
darkness."[55] We struggled to make our way through dense
patches of bamboo grass. We forded streams, and we
stumbled over stones. Dripping with a cold sweat, we
came out at last on the Mogami plain. The young man
who had guided us said, "I have never made this crossing
without something happening. We have really done something wonderful to get here without trouble." We parted
amid rejoicing on both sides and later heard confirmation
of what the guide had said. It made us tremble to think of
what we had gone through.

At Obanazawa we inquired after a man called Seifū
who, though a rich merchant, had no vulgarity in him.[56]
He had often been to and from the capital and so knew
what wayfaring was like. He pressed us to stay with him

---

[55] From *Chêng fu ma ch'en huo t'o yen tung chung.*
[56] Suzuki Seifū (1651–1721) of the Shimadaya. The first two sentences
reflect feudal prejudice against merchants, as well as the way merchants
rose above it, commonly by following the cultivated pursuits of the military aristocracy, from which Bashō himself came.

for a few days—to refresh ourselves after the rigors of so long a journey—and took all manner of good care of us. I wrote some verses while staying with him.

> I sit for a spell,[57]
> Taking the coolness as my house,
> Idling in comfort.

> Come, jump out, there—
> Under the silkworm nursery,
> The croak of a toad.

> Taking its image
> From a little cosmetic brush,
> Flowering rouge-thistle.

Sora added:

> Minding their silkworms,
> People keep the simple appearance
> Of ages long past.

In the fief of Yamagata there is a mountain temple called Ryushaku. Established by the Great Teacher Jikaku,[58] it is situated in an area of great quiet and evident purity. Having been urged to visit it, we set out off our main course from Obanazawa, the distance being some fifteen miles. It was still afternoon when we arrived. Arranging with the priests for temple lodgings at the foot of the mountain, we ascended the slope to the temple proper. The mountain seemed to be built up of rocks upon boulders. The pines and oaks were manifestly old, and the very stones and earth, lying under their smooth shroud of moss, gave off an atmosphere of great age. The doors of

---

[57] "I sit for a spell," etc. The poem uses some dialect. "Come, crawl out, there," etc. That the toads are intended to be poetic can be understood by the fact that two love poems lie behind this: *MYS*, X: 2,265 and XVI: 3,818. "Taking its image," etc. Rouge-thistle is an aster resembling a thistle; its flowers are used for make-up, and this lies behind Bashō's association. Seifū was a merchant dealing with these flowers (which had other commercial value as well), a product of the area. "Minding their silkworms," etc. The appearance is probably that of bent peasant forms in clothing traditional for the work.

[58] Jikaku (794–865) is said to have founded the temple in 860 on the commission of Emperor Seiwa (r. 858–876).

the temple pavilion up there on the rocks were all barred. There was not so much as a sound. Coasting around the brink of the grounds, as if we were creeping over the stones, we paid a manner of worship at the temple, but it was the scenery that struck a stillness in our hearts, purifying them from worldly defilement.

> In seclusion, silence.
> Shrilling into the mountain boulder,
> The cicada's rasp.

Deciding to board a boat down the Mogami River, we went to a place called Ōishida and awaited fair weather. During the delay, someone from the area told us "the seeds of *haikai* sown in this place long ago continue to grow, but we cannot forget how the art flowered here in former times and long for such success again. Minds as simple as ours could use instruction in an art more elegant than our piping on reed flutes. As far as understanding the central principles of this art are concerned, we grope along with our feet, losing our way between new ways and old. We are guideless and perplexed. We certainly do not wish to let pass the opportunity given by your visit." They would not take no for an answer. We composed a sheaf of poems with them, leaving it behind. In such fashion my journey has allowed the style I practice to become known even in so remote an area as this.

The Mogami River begins in Michinoku Province, and its upper reaches mark the boundary of Yamagata. In the middle of its course there are such hazardous places as Goten and Hayabusa. Thereafter it flows along the northern side of Mount Itajiki and empties into the sea at Sakata. Along both its banks the mountains rose upon us as if to close over the river, and the vegetation was wildly luxuriant. Yet through such passage boats drop downstream towards the sea. Was it not because they carried rice that they were called riceboats in our older poetry? We passed Shiraito Falls cascading among a cluster of freshly leaved trees, and the Pavilion of the Immortals standing hard by

Fig. 17. Opening Sheet of *The Verse Record of My Peonies*
From Botan Kuroku Sasshi *(see the Bibliographical Note).*
A gift to the translator from Mr. and Mrs. Saihei Nakagawa

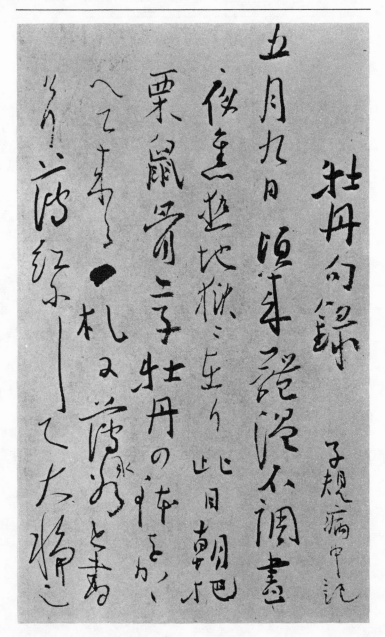

Fɪɢ. 18. Masaoka Shiki Late in His Brief Life

From a portrait by Nakamura Fusetsu,
who appears in the diary.

Courtesy of Kadokawa Shoten

the river. The swollen current rages along, a certain danger to our boat plying on.

> The summer rains
> Collected in a surging current:
> The Mogami River.

The third of the Sixth Month, we climbed Mount Haguro. We inquired after a man called Zushi Sakichi and, with his good offices, met the auxiliary bishop, Egaku,[59] a man of unusual warmth. He put us up in an outlying temple, the Minamidani, and treated us to a banquet.

The fourth there was a gathering for composing *haikai* at the main seat of the temple. My opening verses ran:

> How gratifying it is—
> Snow patches fragrant in the summer wind
> At Minamidani.[60]

The fifth we worshiped at Haguro Gongen. It is not at all clear when its founder, the Great Teacher Nōjo, lived.[61] It appears in the *Engi Rites* as "The Shrine of Ushū Satoyama." But that must be the result of some copyist's mistaking the similar characters, *sato* and *kuro*. Moreover, Ushū Kuroyama must have arisen from the omission of the *-shu* and changing the pronunciation of *u* to *ha*: Haguroyama. The reason the province is called Dewa, or Producing of Feathers, is, according to the *Fudoki*,[62] that the plumage of birds was sent from here to the court. With Gassan and Yudono, Mount Haguro is one of the three principal temples of the area and an affiliate of Kan'ei Temple back in Edo. It is a place where the discipline of concentration and insight practiced in Tendai Buddhism

---

[59] Sakichi (d. 1693) was a *haikai* poet; Egaku (d. 1707) an acting bishop. The 3rd of the Sixth Month is July 19 by our calendar.

[60] Sora's *Diary* makes clear that the poem as composed on the journey (like some others) originally ran differently. The first version may be rendered, ". . . The snow patches given a fragrance / By the sound of the wind." There is an echo of a Chinese poem in a popular collection of the time.

[61] Nōjo is said to be the third son of Emperor Sushun (r. 587–592).

[62] In Bashō's time reference books falsely attributed the explanation to the *Fudoki*. Dewa is the Japanese name for the province, and Ushū the Sinified.

has brightened the world like the moon and where, in addition, the doctrine of Enlightenment Through Tranquility in the Law has been like an accompanying lamp in the night. The priests' quarters consist of a row of buildings where the ascetics diligently practice various forms of discipline. People value the efficacy of this holy mountain and restrain their fears. Its success deserves to continue and to keep the area a center for such admirable good work.

The eighth we climbed Mount Gassan. It entailed wrapping of scarves about our bodies, putting on headdresses of bound cotton strips, calling on all our strength to guide us as we climbed up the almost twenty miles. We walked in snow and ice in a cold mountain atmosphere among the clouds and mists, as if in the high heavens beside the paths of the sun and moon. It was an agony to breathe, and our bodies seemed to mutter against us. But at last we reached the summit, finding that the sun had set and the moon was risen. Arranging for a place to sleep, we spread out bamboo grass, with fine bamboos for a pillow. It was on such beds that we waited out the night. When the sun rose and melted away the clouds, we descended to Yudono.

Here Gassan the swordsmith chose the waters of the area for their miraculous tempering power.[63] Purifying himself in them, his mind and body made right, he would hammer out a sword. When he put "Gassan" to a masterwork, it was something the world would treasure. In China they used to temper swords in the waters of Lung-chüan Spring, and the waters chosen here by Gassan are of that order of excellence. He was a person who admired such figures as Kan Chiang and his wife Mo-yeh of the Wu dynasty, they who made the famous swords to which they gave their own names, and he well understood how little common was the dedication necessary to make outstanding things.

While sitting down on a stone to rest, I noticed a cherry tree only three feet high and about half blossomed out. Although it is buried by the snow that piles up so deeply here, this late blossomer does not forget the spring, and I found its spirit touching. It is as though the plum blossoms in dead summer that one reads of in Chinese verse were giving off

---

[63] Gassan flourished in the late eleventh century.

their fragrance here, or as if the touching cherry tree that Bishop Gyōson wrote of had blossomed again, and such recollections make this tree seem yet more precious.[64]

The customary discipline of pilgrims does not allow me to give a detailed description of the area around Mount Yudono, and more than that, we are not even to write of it. Returning from Gassan to our lodging at Minamidani, at the urging of Egaku we wrote out on poem cards some of the verses we had composed in our walking tour of the three mountains of Dewa.

> How cool it is—
> The crescent moon seen faintly
> On Mount Haguro.[65]

> The peak of clouds
> Forms and crumbles, forms and crumbles—
> But Gassan in moonlight!

> No one may relate
> The mysteries of Mount Yudono;
> Yet tears wet my sleeves.

And Sora:

> My tears fall on the path
> As I tread the unregarded offerings
> Of Mount Yudono temples.

We left Mount Haguro and went to the castle town of Tsurugaoka, where we were taken to the house of Naga-yama Shigeyuki,[66] a samurai, and there composed a set of *haikai*. Sakichi was also there to see us off as we boarded

---

[64] Gyōson (1057–1135) was a Tendai ecclesiastic; the poem Bashō alludes to speaks of a mountain cherry like this, far from the sight of men: *KYS*, IX: 556.

[65] "The peak of clouds," etc. Contrasting day and night scenes, cloud peaks and actual mountain, the original plays on *Tsuki no yama*, both meaning the mountain in moonlight and giving the Japanese reading for "Gassan" (Moon-mountain). "No one may relate," etc. Referring to the rules about not describing the area. For his part, Bashō can also not explain, only show that he was moved. "My tears fall," etc. Sora's *Diary* records that there were so many offerings that they blew about on the paths, apparently ignored by the ascetics.

[66] Shigeyuki (dates unknown) was a poet of Bashō's school. It is believed that Sakichi (see n. 59), mentioned in the next sentence, was somehow connected with Shigeyuki and had accompanied Bashō as far as Tsurugaoka.

the boat for Sakata Harbor. We took lodging at the house of a physician who had taken En'an Fugyoku[67] as his poetic name.

> Southwards Mount Atsumi,
> Then looking north to breezy Fuku Bay,
> And the cool of the evening.

> The River Mogami,
> Thrusts the sun and ends the day's heat
> In the cooling sea.

Whether rivers or hills, sea or land, the scenery we had already looked upon had been magnificent. Now my heart urged me to look at Kisa Bay.[68] We walked northeast from the port of Sakata, crossing mountains, limping along rocky shores, swishing across sandy beaches, and covering well over twenty miles, and that just as at last the sun was sinking brightly to the west, as the strong onshore breeze stirred up the sand, and as the rain threw into a dim haze the islands, the sea, and Mount Chōkai. The rain cast a darkness over the scenery, and I felt as though I were groping in shadows. But it is "a landscape also of special beauty when veiled by the rain," and we could hope for another surpassing view when the veil of rain had lifted. With such thoughts we barely squeezed into "a fisherman's reed hut / On Kisa Bay."[69]

The next morning the sky was very clear and, just as the sun was shining its brightest, we set our boat upon the bay. We headed for Nōin Isle, where we inquired after some sign of the place where Priest Nōin had lived so peacefully for three years. Then we crossed back to the shore of the mainland to the place famous for the cherry tree of Priest

---

[67] Fugyoku (d. 1697) had joined Bashō's poetic school after practicing other styles.

[68] Kisa Bay is a large inlet about twenty-five miles northeast of Sakata; a famous beauty spot, it has about a hundred islands within it and there were then about thirty towns along its coast.

[69] The beauty of scenery veiled or unveiled by rain recalls a poem by Su Tung-p'o, *Yin hu-shang ch'u ch'ing hou yü*, in which he also compares the scene to the beauty of Lady Hsi-shih, who was voluptuous with either little or heavy cosmetics, as Bashō suggests in his next poem. See also n. 72. The sublimity of the prose in the paragraph characteristically concludes with a humble reed hut, echoing a poem of Priest Nōin, *GSIS*, IX: 519.

Saigyō's poem, and saw an aged tree, a keepsake of Saigyō.[70] By the coast there is an imperial mausoleum, which
is said to be that of Empress Jingū.[71] The temple of the
area is Kanmanju. I had never heard before that Empress
Jingū had visited the area. What is one to make of the
story? Seated in the banquet room of this temple, with the
reed lattice rolled up, we could see a wide panorama lying
before us. To the south, islands, the sea, and Mount Chōkai looming up to support the heavens and reflected below
in the waters of Kisa Bay. To the west, the Muyamuya
Barrier cuts across the road, and to the east there runs an
embankment and far beyond it, dim in the distance, the
road to Akita. Again, off to the north, where the surf seems
to draw the sea back and forth, is a place called Shiogoshi.
Kisa Bay extends more than two miles each way. It re-
minds me of Matsushima, but with this difference: Matsushima carried an air of people smiling; Kisa Bay suggests
rather the gloom of a frown. It is not just that it is melancholy—more than that, there is an impression of pain, and
the effect is that of a beautiful woman whose heart is sorely
troubled.

> Pink flowering silk-trees,
> Dimmed in the rain like the beauty of Hsi Shih,
> The Bay of Kisa.[72]

---

[70] The poem was then thought to be by Saigyō:
> At the Bay of Kisa
> The cherry tree is buried under
> The lapping ocean waves,
> And the little boats of fisherfolk
> Row along above the blossoms.

[71] Empress Jingū was queen of Emperor Chūai and regent from 201
to 269. But dates that early are very suspect and her association with the
area was wholly legendary, as Bashō's skepticism suggests. Cf. n. 102,
below.

[72] "Pink-flowering silk trees," etc. The beauty of the scene is compared
to the beauty of Hsi Shih, lovely even in frowns; she was sent as a
present to Kou-chien of the Yüeh by Fu-chai of the Wu dynasty.
"The Bay of Kisa," etc. The place was famous for its shellfish. Sora
wonders what more festive food the village could turn to. Little is known
of Teiji, though he was a merchant with the surname Miyabe and is
thought to have been from Gifu (near modern Nagoya), where Bashō
may have met him and taken him into his school. "Waves will not wash
it," etc. Washing waves represent betrayal in love in court poetry, and
Sora alludes to an anonymous Eastern Song, KKS, XX: 1,093. See *The
Diary of Izumi Shikibu*, nn. 17 and 18.

> At Shiogoshi Inlet:
> Cranes wetting spindly legs in the shallows,
> The sea breathing coolness.

Sora wrote some verses at the time of the summer festival there.

> The Bay of Kisa—
> What special food can be eaten
> On festival day?

Teiji, a merchant from Mino Province, wrote:

> The fisher huts—
> Their rain shutters taken off for benches
> In the cool of the evening.

And Sora wrote upon seeing two ospreys nesting on a rock,

> Waves will not wash it:
> There is the fond bond of husband and wife
> In the nest of the osprey.

A number of days passed in our taking leave of the people of Sakata, but at last we turned our attention to the cloud-covered road to the south along this far side of the country. The thought of the distance to be covered makes one's heart ache—I hear that it is more than 280 miles to the capital of Kaga Province. But we set out, crossing the Nezu Barrier, set foot in the province of Echigo for the first time, and at last reached the Ichiburi Barrier into Etchū Province. During the nine days of that stage, my spirits were greatly afflicted by the heat and the wet weather, and since my illness broke out again, that part of my travel record must be left vacant.

> First month of autumn—
> This eve of the Seventh-Night Festival
> Is unlike other nights.[73]

---

[73] "First month of autumn," etc. It is the Seventh Month of the lunar calendar; on the Tanabata Festival of the 7th, see *The Diary of Izumi Shikibu*, n. 26. "The wild ocean," etc. Sado lies off the coast of Niigata city. "The river of stars" is the Milky Way. The vast panorama and the force of nature suggest the insignificance of man.

> The wild dark ocean:
> Streaming over it to Sado Island,
> The river of stars.

Today we passed the most trying part of our north-country journey, going through dangerous places with such horrible names as Deserting-Parents–Abandoned-Children, Excluded Dog, and Rejected Horse. I was so tired that I searched out a pillow and lay down as soon as I could. Two young women were talking, however, in the next room but one, toward the front of the building. Mingled with their voices was that of an old man, and from what was said I understood that the women were from Niigata in Echigo Province, and that they were prostitutes. They were on their way to worship at the Ise Shrine, and the man had come to see them as far as this barrier at Ichiburi. He would go back to Niigata tomorrow, while they were writing letters and giving him various broken messages to carry back.

The conversation floated to me. "We are as they say waves falling upon the beach, coming to ruin on the shore, expecting no better end than 'fisherwomen' like us ever have. People treat us with disgust, and we fall lower and lower. Each night we are pledged to love a different man. To have to endure such a shameful life, what terrible things must we have done in a previous existence?"

I fell to sleep with their words in my ears, and just as we were setting out the next morning, the two women came up to us weeping.

"We don't know what route to take," they said, "and so we are terribly worried about our trip. Our anxiety has made us miserable about what lies ahead, and we wonder, may we follow you—at a distance far enough so we would not embarrass you? Your clothes show that you are priests, and that means you will have pity. The boundless grace of the Buddha can be bestowed even on such as we, so please help our souls to enter his Way." They continued in tears as they spoke.

"I regret it very much," I told them, "but we are not so much traveling anywhere as stopping here and there for periods of time. It would really be better for you if you accompanied ordinary travelers. The favor of the gods should enable you to get to Ise without trouble." With that we set out on our way, but the great pity of their situation troubled me for some time.

> Prostitutes and priest
> Slept under a roof lent a beauty
> By bush clover and moon.[74]

I spoke out the verses to Sora, who set them down in his *Diary*.

They say that the Kurobe has forty-eight rapids, and although I do not know how many rivers we crossed, we came at last to a bay called Nago. We were told that while it was not the proper spring season for seeing the famous wisteria at nearby Tako, the place was still worth a look in early autumn. When we asked where it was, we were told, "Well, you would have to go about twelve miles along the coast and so into that area hidden by the mountains. There are only a few miserable huts of fishermen, and you probably would not be able to obtain lodging for the night." Intimidated by that, we walked on to Kaga Province.

> The ripening grain,
> Walking in the fragrance while on the right
> The rocky shore of the sea.

Crossing Mount Unohana and the Pass of Kurikara, we arrived in Kanazawa on the fifteenth of the Seventh Month. We encountered a merchant with the *haikai* name of Kasho,[75] traveling here from Osaka, and we shared lodgings with him. There was a man of these parts, Isshō,[76] who was,

---

[74] The flowering bush clover symbolizes the women as the moon does the poet-priest. The poem is esteemed for the kinship, beauty, and pathos it implies Bashō found in the encounter. It is not in Sora's *Diary* and therefore was written later, probably, as the Introduction to this book suggests, to have a love episode after the manner of a "love-verse" in linked poetry.

[75] Kasho (d. 1731) was a follower of Bashō's school.

[76] Although a provincial poet, Kosugi Isshō (1653–1688) was very

I had heard, devoted to the art of poetry. His name as a writer was increasingly heard, and many who were not themselves poets had come to know of him. I discovered that he had died last winter, and now his elder brother proposed a memorial service at which we would compose elegiac verse.

> Shake, little grave mound!
> The voice with which I cry is at one
> With the autumn wind.

And on being invited to a thatched hermitage:

> Autumn is cool now—
> Let us peel a feast with both hands,
> Melon and eggplant.

There were others composed on the road.

> Crimson on red,
> The sun sets with yet remaining heat,
> But autumn is in the wind.

At a place called Komatsu,

> How nice it sounds,
> This name, Komatsu, where wind ruffles over
> The bush clover and pampas.

We paid a visit to the Tada Shrine here in Komatsu. The helmet and part of the fabric of the armor of Sanemori are preserved in the shrine.[77] I was told that these things were presented to Sanemori long ago, while he still adhered to the Minamoto cause, by Lord Yoshitomo.[78] Certainly they were not the possessions of any ordinary samurai. The visor

---

talented and was one of the first to practice Bashō's mature style successfully. The two poets must have been eager for the meeting they were denied, as Bashō's passionate elegy shows.

[77] Saitō Sanemori (1111–1183), killed at the battle of Shinohara in the area Bashō was visiting, had dyed his white hair so as not to be dissuaded from, or derided in, battle. He had changed allegiance from the Minamoto to the losing Taira in the Gempei Wars, and his is a story of loss in many ways.

[78] Minamoto Yoshitomo (1147–1199) was father of Yoritomo, who founded Minamoto rule of the country, and of the legendary tragic Yoshitsune.

and the earflaps were laterally engraved and inlaid with gold arabesque of a chrysanthemum pattern. A goldwork dragon ornamented the crown, and at the front of the crown were the hoe-shaped crests on either side. The records describe with great vividness the events of those times, telling how Kiso no Yoshinaka had grieved over Sanemori and sent these two possessions to the shrine along with a letter of supplication.[79] Higuchi Jirō was said to be the bearer of these relics. I wrote some verses reflecting on the story.

> What a loss is here:
> Beneath the warrior's splendid helmet
> A chirping cricket.

On our way to Yamanaka Hot Springs, the peak of Shirane regarded us from behind as we walked along.[80] At the bottom of a mountain on our left we came upon a temple of Kannon. After Cloistered Emperor Kazan had visited the Kannons of thirty-three places in succession, he had this statue of the great Bodhisattva of Mercy installed, and it is said that it was he who gave the temple its name, Nata, made up from parts of "Nachi" and "Tanigumi."[81] The rocks on the slopes of the temple are varied in shape. Pines now grown old were planted along them, and little reed-thatched temples have been perched on the rocky outcroppings. Altogether it is a fine place.

> These stones excel
> The stones of Ishiyama in whiteness:
> The autumn wind.[82]

---

79 Minamoto Yoshinaka (1154–1184), brought up in Kiso, was a skillful but inflammatory general on the Minamoto side during the Gempei Wars. He was killed by Yoritomo's troops when he rebelled. Higuchi Jirō, or Kanemitsu, mentioned a bit later, was one of Yoshinaka's four famous lieutenants and died with him in battle.

80 Shirane, or Shirayama, is one of the three most famous mountains of Japan and separated three of the ancient provinces in what is now the area of Ishikawa Prefecture.

81 Emperor Kazan (r. 984–986) abdicated to religious life at the age of eighteen. Nachi and Tanigumi are places in present Wakayama and Gifu Prefectures, the former the first, the latter the last, of the thirty-three temples visited by Kazan and so appropriate as the basis for the name of his temple.

82 "The stones of Ishiyama," etc. These verses have aroused a great

We took the waters of the spa. Their efficacy is said to rival the waters of Ariake.[83]

> At Yamanaka—
> Asters cannot match the fragrance
> Of the life-giving waters.[84]

The master of the hot springs lodge is called Kumenosuke, and he is still a youngster.[85] His father[86] had a taste for *haikai*, and years ago when Teishitsu of the capital visited here while still a fledgling poet, he was so put to shame by the performance of this lad's father that he returned to the capital, became a pupil of Teitoku, and so gradually became known to the world. They say that after he grew famous he took for his poetic teaching no fees from people of this one remote village. Of course all this is a tale of events long ago.

Sora has fallen ill with abdominal trouble. Because he has relatives at Nagashima in Ise, he is going ahead alone.

> Walking, walking on,
> Though I collapse I shall be buried
> On a bush-clover plain.[87]

He wrote down the verses and left them with me. There are the sufferings of the one who goes, and the unhappi-

---

deal of discussion. The most widely accepted version of their meaning is that though the famous Ishiyama Temple near Lake Biwa has famous white stones, those are not as white as those of this hill of stones (*ishiyama*). Bashō's grammar is slightly ambiguous, suggesting a whiteness to the autumn wind, as in such a court poem as that by Fujiwara Teika (1162–1241), *SKKS*, XV: 1,336.

[83] Ariake is thought to be a mistake for Arima, near what is now Kobe City.

[84] The poem refers to a Chinese legend about a large aster or chrysanthemum bedewed with drops of sweet water conducive to long life.

[85] Kumenosuke, or Izumiya Matabē (1676–1751), about thirteen years old when Bashō made his visit.

[86] The father (d. 1679) also had the business name of Izumiya Matabē. The Teishitsu whom he embarrassed was Yasuhara Masahira (1610–1673) a distinguished *haikai* poet of the school of Matsunaga Teitoku (1570–1653).

[87] Some editors see an allusion in this poem to Saigyō's poem from his personal collection, *Sankashū, Zoku Kokka Taikan*, 7,837.

ness of him left behind, each like one of two wild ducks lost from each other.[88] I responded with verses.

> From today the dew
> Will erase the inscription on my hat,
> "I travel with a friend."[89]

I have stopped at a temple called Zenshō on the outskirts of the castle town of Daishōji. This is still Kaga Province. Sora had stopped here the night before and left a poem behind.

> Throughout the night,
> Sleeplessly listening to the autumn wind—
> Parted and in hills remote.

"Parted for a night, parted for a thousand leagues."[90] I too heard that autumn wind as I lay in the same temple dormitory, and when dawn began to brighten the sky, the voices of priests at their morning recitations came distinct to my ear. After a time the assembly bell rang for breakfast, and I joined the priests in their dining hall. Thinking that I had to get into Echizen Province today, I felt rather in a hurry, but as I started down the steps from the dining hall, young priests crowded about me, holding out paper and an inkstone. It happened to be the time when the willows of the temple garden were dropping their leaves, so I wrote:

> The willow leaves fall—
> After sweeping the temple garden
> I hope I can leave.[91]

Anxious to get on, I just scribbled it down, as if my sandals were already in motion.

---

[88] Faithful wild ducks were emblems of close friends or married pairs.

[89] Bashō and Sora had evidently followed the traveler's custom, when making up a pair, of writing on their bamboo hats, "I am one of two journeying together."

[90] The expression was proverbial in Chinese poems.

[91] The poem alludes to the custom of one's performing some menial task like cleaning a room or garden before leaving a Zen temple where one had spent the night. Bashō seems the more human for his irritation with the young priests.

At Yoshizaki on the border of Echizen Province I took to a boat and was rowed across the inlet to look at the pines of Shiogoshi.[92]

> All through the night
> The waves have been borne ashore
> By the furious wind,
> And the moonlight sparkled in the water
> Dripping from the Shiogoshi pines.
>
> —SAIGYŌ[93]

The poem has been posted on behalf of numerous views in this area. Adding a line or even a word to its five lines would be as superfluous as adding a sixth finger to one's hand.[94]

The head priest of Tenryū Temple in Maruoka was a man with whom I had had connections for a very long time, and so it was that I visited him. There was also a man named Hokushi from Kanazawa, who had promised to see me off from his city, but he gradually lengthened his time with me until now we were here at this temple together.[95] All along the way he was reluctant to pass by any place of special beauty without composing verse, and from time to time he recited for me several excellent poems. Now that we were parting at last, I wrote a poem for him.

> Scribbled all over,
> The summer fan might be rejected now,
> But for its memories.[96]

About fifty blocks, as it were, from the town, I turned into the hills and went to worship at Eihei Temple. It was founded by the Zen Priest Dōgen.[97] Wishing, as a devout

---

[92] Shiogoshi, on the Japan Sea side of the island, was famous for its stand of fifty or so pines; from there Bashō heads south.

[93] The poem is not really by Saigyō.

[94] Bashō echoes *Chuang Tzu*, Chap. VIII.

[95] Tachibana Hokushi (d. 1718) was a poet of Bashō's school. The temple mentioned is in Matsuoka, not Maruoka, which is nearby.

[96] A fan is no longer needed in the cooler weather of autumn, yet in spite of being scribbled on, it is precious for its associations. It is a metaphor for Hokushi, and for Bashō's reluctance to part.

[97] Priest Dōgen (1200–1253) was founder of Sōtō Zen Buddhism.

priest might well do, to avoid the attractions of the capital, he came off to this forsaken place in the hills, leaving worldly affairs behind.

Because Fukui lies only about six and a half miles away, I set out after finishing the evening meal. In the twilight the road was uncertain underfoot. There is a cultivated samurai named Tōsai living here.[98] Many years ago now he came to Edo and called on me—it must be above ten years past. I thought that he must be very aged by this time, or even dead, but when I asked people about him they said that, no, he was still quite alive and told me where I might find him. It turned out to be a place secluded in the center of town, a shabby little structure but delightfully overgrown with moonflowers and gourd vines, its entrance all but hidden by a profusion of cockscomb and broom tree. I said to myself, "This *has* to be the place." I knocked at the entrance and there appeared a woman of the most ragged appearance. "Where do you come from, Your Reverence?" she asked. "The man of the house has gone to the place of Mr. What-ever-it-was nearby. If you want to speak with him, you had best inquire there." Her manner suggested that she was Tōsai's wife.

Thinking that such beauty in an unpromising place was like some tale of old,[99] I at last inquired after Tōsai and stayed with him two nights. I told him that I thought the harbor of Tsuruga would be a good place to see the autumn moon and started to take my leave. At that Tōsai said he would accompany me and, tucking up the hem of his kimono into his sash, he started off with a jaunty air to guide me.

As we walked on, I found that the imposing peak of Shirane was at last screened from sight, and the top of Mount

---

[98] Kambe or Sugiura Tōsai (d. 1700) was an important *haikai* poet of the Teitoku school.

[99] Talk of "some tale of old" brings to the surface the recollection of the Yūgao chapter of *The Tale of Genji*, which underlies the whole Fukui episode and in which there is the remark, "You hear of such things in tales of old."

Hina stood out clearly. We crossed Asamuzu Bridge, and upon arriving at Tamae found that its famous reeds were headed out.[100] We passed Uguisu Barrier by the side, crossed over Yunō Pass, and on Mount Kaeru near the ruins of Hiuchi Castle I heard the first geese coming south. At dusk on the evening of the autumn full moon, I took lodgings at the harbor of Tsuruga.

The moon was splendid that night. When I asked, "Can we hope to see the moon like this tomorrow night?" my host told me, "Given the changeable nature of the weather in this area, it is difficult to predict a fair or cloudy night."[101] He poured me sake and, at his suggestion, we paid a night visit to the Myōjin shrine at Kei, which honors Emperor Chūai.[102] The shrine had an aura of divinity, and down upon it poured the moonlight between the trees onto the white sand, making it look as if a thick frost had spread over all.

My host told me, "Long ago, the second Archabbot observed the ordeal faced by worshipers at this shrine, and he himself cut away plants, carried earth and sand, gathered the marshy waters into a pool, and so tidied the area that worshipers needed fear no discomfort.[103] This ancient example has lasted on as an unbroken tradition, and still today you will see sand carried into the shrine. It is called 'The Archabbot's Sand-bearing.' " I wrote some verses.

> Divinely pure,
> The moonlight sparkles on the sand
> Borne by the Archabbot.

Just as my host had foretold, it rained the next night.

---

100 The reeds of Tamae were famous enough, but the whole passage is built into a *michiyuki*, or travel passage with beautiful names (e.g., Uguisu Barrier, the Barrier of the Warbler) and associations, a technique common in a number of Japanese literary forms.

101 The implication, sanctioned by proverbs from the Chinese and Japanese past, is to enjoy the moon on the clear night before, even though it is not wholly full.

102 Emperor Chūai is said to be the fourteenth emperor of Japan and to have ruled 192–200. Cf. n. 71, above.

103 Bashō varies from other accounts; editors say that the event took place in 1301, and that the second archabbot died in 1319.

In the north country
The night of the full autumn moon,
Untrustworthy weather.

The next day, the sixteenth, the sky had cleared, and thinking that I would like to look for the famous little colored clams, I took a boat to the Beach of Iro.[104] It is a passage of about fifteen miles. A man called Tenya Something-or-other went with me, his servants taking an ample provision of lunchboxes and sake flasks.[105] We settled in the boat and set off with a smart wind, arriving in no time at all. On the beach, where there were but few huts of fishermen, there was a pitiable little Nichiren temple. It was there that we sat, and as we drank tea, heating and drinking sake, I felt the particular melancholy of an autumn evening.

The lonely sadness,
Exceeding even that of Suma Beach,
These shores of autumn.

In intervals of surf,
The little colored shells are jumbled
With bush-clover rubbish.[106]

At my request, Tōsai wrote an outline of the events of the day and left it at the temple.

Rotsū met me as I was going back to Tsuruga Harbor, and from there accompanied me to Mino Province.[107] Our pace quickened by going on horseback, it was not long be-

---

[104] The clams are those made famous by Saigyō's poem, Sankashū, Zoku Kokka Taikan, 8,189.

[105] Tenya Gorōzaemon (dates unknown) was a haikai poet. The passage is actually about four miles.

[106] The two poems vary greatly, the first being subjective and allusive to the sadness of Suma Beach (from The Tale of Genji and other stories), the second, objective with its image of bits of broken bush-clover mingling with the famous shells.

[107] The names of a number of Bashō's friends and pupils follow. Yasomura or Inbe Rotsū (1648–1738) was in Bashō's school. Ochi Etsujin (d. ca. 1739) was a prominent member of it. Kondō Jōkō entered it in 1687. Tsuda Zensen (dates unknown) belonged, as did also Miyazaki Keikō (d. 1693) and his three sons. As in haikai or renga linked verse, the passage of time speeds up just before the last verse, a great distance and many people being covered here.

fore we entered the town of Ōgaki, where Sora had arrived from Ise and where Etsujin had also hurried in by
horse. We all gathered at Jokō's house. Master Zensen,
Keikō and his sons, and many others among my close
friends came, by day and by night. They looked upon me
as if I had come back from the dead, sympathized with
me for the hardships of travel, and rejoiced with me that
I had come through. The strain of travel still weighed upon
me. But because it was already the sixth of the Ninth
Month, I resolved to get on to observe the rare ceremonies
at the Great Shrines of Ise.[108] And so, boarding a boat yet
again—

> Parting for Futami Bay
> Is like tearing the body from the clam-shell:
> Autumn goes to its end.[109]

---

[108] The rare ceremonies, which were held every twenty-one years, took
place on the 10th and 13th of the Ninth Month of 1689.

[109] Futami Bay is near the Ise Shrines, but *Futami* may also be taken
as shell-body.

The Verse Record
of My Peonies
(Botan Kuroku)
by Masaoka Shiki

The Verse Record of My Peonies

A Diary of an Illness

May 9th.

With my temperature irregularly high recently, my days and nights have become a hell of fire. This morning Haritsu and Sokotsu[1] have come by, bringing a pot of peonies. On the name tag was written, "Thin Ice." They have large flowers, light vermilion in color. At night Kyoshi[2] arrived, bringing Western-style food. I took medicine twice in the daytime and twice at night, but although exhausted by excessive sweating, I fell asleep with difficulty.

> Here in tissue paper
> Is the parcel of flowers:
> The peonies.

> Borne here to me
> On a jinrikisha, the peonies
> Still swaying.

> The gift brought me
> Is peonies tended in a pot:
> Just so my illness.

> Glowing brightly,
> A single flower of the peonies
> Lights up the sickroom.

> Critical now,
> Bedridden with illness:
> The peony flowers.

[1] Like most of the people mentioned, Fukuda Haritsu (b. 1865) and Samukawa Sokotsu (b. 1875) are disciples of Shiki.

[2] Takahama Kyoshi (1874–1959), Shiki's best-known disciple.

It lies beneath
The framed writing of Lord Masamune:[3]
The pot of peonies.

Decked in the rainhat
And straw raincoat of an itinerant poet:
Peonies in an old house.

Tonight I heard my first wood thrush of the year.

In the alcove
The darkness of the peonies:
The wood thrush sings.

During the day my uncle visited me.

May 10th.

After an enema in the morning I slept a little. I feel
slightly improved.

It is always the case with this affliction of mine that
when May comes:

Month of bad omen
When they blossomed in the garden:
Peony flowers.

The unbearable pain makes me wonder what possesses
me to wish to live on. I wonder, shall I die? Shall I die? I
take a draught of medicine in resignation and, thinking I
will die, know my life to be as precarious as dew. Come
now: it might be worth some amusement to hold the most
splendid celebration of a lifetime—on my Departing This
Life. What I might try is to set a day, make my intent
known to this person and that, and enjoin all the guests
to come with flowers or fruit instead of the usual gifts for
the dead. Soon after all were assembled, each one could
compose an elegiac *haiku*. What a treat it would be to go
through the fruit as it pleased me and, when the time came
that my belly was full there among the mountains of flowers and fruit, take the compound with a good grace and
quietly slip off into endless sleep.[4]

---

[3] For Masamune, see Bashō, *The Narrow Road*, n. 42.

[4] A note to this paragraph in the *Shiki Zenshū* version (see the Bibliographical Note) says, "This paragraph was recorded by Saemon."
Saemon appears a bit later (see n. 5); Shiki was obviously too ill to write.

Why not die then,
In front of the peony flowers,
Eating up apples?

There is this silence
About the sickbed as the petals
Drop from the peonies!

Two flakes fall
And the shape of the peonies
Is wholly changed.

Hyōtei came by in the morning. Saemon came in the afternoon and the painter Fusetsu in the evening.[5] The paper cover of these sheets has become a picture with the falling blossoms.

May 11th.

In the morning Katsuō and Teiken came by.[6] Not a one of the peony blossoms this morning but was fallen.

The peonies have fallen,
And what alone is left behind
Is—Bashō's portrait!

It occurred to me to set aside one large petal from the peonies, but the children got at the fallen blossoms and soon made an end of them.

I took my temperature tonight and discovered it to be almost 104°. Recently it has risen twice a day, as it did yesterday. But today, as formerly, it rose only once.

In three days' time
The peony blossoms are ended:
My record in verse.

---

[5] Iwaki Hyōtei (1870–1939); Yoshino Dazaemon or Saemon (1877–1920); and Nakamura Fusetsu (dates unknown).

[6] Surnames and dates are unknown for Katsuō and Teiken.

Bibliographical Note

Bibliographical Note

The intention of this note is to specify those works drawn upon most frequently for the translation, those of immediate use for background or assessment, and those in English, primarily translations, that may prove of interest to the reader. For detailed bibliographical assistance, the reader should consult the Japanese editions and studies listed. The editions used for text, though not always as prime source for interpretation, have been starred. Unless specified, the place of publication is Tokyo.

General Works

Akiyama Ken, *et al.* (eds.). *Heian Nikki.* 1960, 1964. In *Kokugo Kokubungaku Kenkyūshi Taisei*, Vol. V. Especially valuable for its reviews of scholarship.

Imai Takauji. *Heian Jidai Nikki Bungaku no Kenkyū.* 1957. A useful work, but mostly superseded by Tamai's study (q.v.).

Tamai Kōsuke. *Nikki Bungaku no Kenkyū.* 1965. The most thorough and up-to-date study of diary literature from 935 to 1350.

The Tosa Diary

Hagitani Boku (ed.). *Tosa Nikki Zenchūshaku.* 1967. A very detailed commentary but published after completion of the manuscript of this book.

Konishi Jin'ichi (ed.). *Tosa Nikki Hyōkai.* 1951. Reprinted well over twenty times. It contains most valuable commentary and original criticism.

*Suzuki Tomotarō, *et al.* (eds). *Tosa Nikki,* etc. 1957. In *Nihon Koten Bungaku Taikei,* Vol. XX. Excellent text and notes, as is usual in this series published by Iwanami Shoten.

Usuda Jingōrō, *et al.* (eds.). *Tosa Nikki* in *Ōchō Nikki.* 1957. In *Nihon Koten Kanshō Kōza,* Vol. VI. Useful commentary, but considerably abridged text.

The Diary of Izumi Shikibu

---

*Endō Yoshimoto (ed.). *Izumi Shikibu Nikki.* 1957. In *Nihon Koten Bungaku Taikei,* Vol. XX. Excellent text and notes.

—————— (ed.). *Shinkō Izumi Shikibu Monogatari.* 1962. A scholarly treatment of a major text, but not the usual copy text, of the *Izumi Shikibu Nikki;* with ample introductory and bibliographical matter.

*Enji Fumiko and Suzuki Kazuo (eds.). *Zenkō Izumi Shikibu Nikki.* 1965. An outstanding edition, the best of many fine ones.

Higashi Setsuo, *et al.* (eds.). *Izumi Shikibu Nikki Sōsakuin.* 1959. Contains two texts in parallel and a word index of some utility.

Omuro Yūzō and Tanaka Eisaburō (eds.). *Izumi Shikibu Nikki Shōkai.* 1957. A very unreliable text but some useful commentary.

Shimizu Fumio (ed.). *Izumi Shikibu Nikki* in *Ōchō Nikki.* 1957. In *Nihon Koten Kanshō Kōza,* Vol. VI. Useful commentary but considerably abridged text.

Yamagishi Tokuhei (ed.). *Izumi Shikibu Nikki.* 1959. In *Nihon Koten Zensho,* Vol. XC. Apart from its high scholarship, interesting for what it reveals by close punctuation and paragraphing.

Yoshida Kōichi. *Izumi Shikibu Kenkyū.* 1964. A very thorough study, sometimes rather speculative, of most aspects of Izumi Shikibu's life and writings.

The Narrow Road Through the Provinces

Imoto Nōichi (ed.). *Oku no Hosomichi* in *Bashō*. 1958. In *Nihon Koten Kanshō Kōza*. Even better commentary than is usual in the series and only one slight abridgment.
*Sugiura Shōichirō, *et al.* (eds.). *Oku no Hosomichi* in *Bashō Bunshū*. 1959. In *Nihon Koten Bungaku Taikei*, Vol. XLVI. The usual excellent text and notes of the series, but more ample commentary than most volumes.

The Verse Record of My Peonies

*Masaoka Shiki. "Botan Kuroku," *Hototogisu*. Vol. IX (June, 1899), pp. 12–13. The first published version.
*————. "Botan Kuroku," *Shiki Zenshū*. 1916. Vol. XIV, 340–342. Has a few variant readings.
*Mori Yūichi (ed.). *Botan Kuroku Sasshi*. Nagoya, 1944. This rare edition includes a facsimile of the original and a printed text, with some comment.
Samukawa Sokotsu. "Shiki Koji no Haiku Kenkyū," *Haiku Kōza*. 1932. Vol. V, 334–342. Commentary of some interest, including reference to a few poems included in *The Verse Record*, by one of the people it mentions.

Translations and Other Useful Works in English

Brower, Robert H., and Earl Miner. *Japanese Court Poetry*. Stanford, 1961. The discussion of the poetry and conventions of courtly love assists in understanding *The Tosa Diary* and *The Diary of Izumi Shikibu*.
Cranston, Edwin Augustus. "*The Izumi Shikibu Nikki*: A Study and Translation." Unpublished doctoral dissertation, Stanford University, 1966. 452 pp.
Keene, Donald. *Japanese Literature: An Introduction for Western Readers*. London, 1953. Also in a paperback edition. A brief but very stimulating book.

———— (ed. and comp.). *Anthology of Japanese Literature*. New York and London, 1955. Also paperback edition. A most useful anthology, including partial translations of *The Tosa Diary* by G. W. Sargent and of *The Narrow Road of Oku* by Donald Keene. Other useful translations for understanding the background of the first three translations are included here.

———— (ed. and comp.). *Modern Japanese Literature*. New York and London, 1956. Also in a paperback edition. Contains some poems by Masaoka Shiki and background useful to understanding the Meiji context of Shiki's diary.

———— (trans.). *Essays in Idleness*. New York and London, 1967. Yoshida Kenkō's *Tsurezuregusa* provides a kind of transition from the world of *The Diary of Izumi Shikibu* to that of *The Narrow Road Through the Provinces*.

McCullough, Helen Craig (trans.). *Tales of Ise*. Stanford, 1968. A translation of the *Ise Monogatari* with authoritative notes and introduction.

Miner, Earl. *Introduction to Japanese Court Poetry*. Stanford, 1968. Places the diary poetry of Tsurayuki and Izumi Shikibu in the larger contexts of their poetry and their age.

Morris, Ivan. *The World of the Shining Prince*. London and New York, 1964. A study of the ethos of "Court Life in Ancient Japan."

———— (trans.). *The Pillow Book of Sei Shōnagon*. 2 vols. New York and London, 1967. Apart from the polished translation of this classic, there is included an abundance of commentary on numerous features of Heian life.

Omori, Annie Shepley and Kochi Doi. *Diaries of Court Ladies of Old Japan*. 1935, 1961. Including *The Sarashina Diary*, *The Diary of Murasaki Shikibu*, and *The Diary of Izumi Shikibu*. Still of some interest, but based on out-dated scholarship and often peculiar in style.

Seidensticker, Edward G. (trans.). *The Gossamer Diary*. 1964. A slightly revised version of *The Kagerō Nikki*, in *Transactions of the Asiatic Society of Japan*. 3d Series,

IV (June, 1955). Of greatest interest for the excellent translation, the Introduction and especially the appendical matter and notes are illuminating on such matters as the architecture and clothes of the period of *The Tosa Diary* and *The Diary of Izumi Shikibu.*

Yuasa, Nobuyuki. *Bashō: The Narrow Road to the Deep North and Other Travel Sketches.* Harmondsworth, England, Penguin Books, 1966. An attractive collection with a useful Introduction and maps.